Praise for Matthew Baylis

'Fabulous and funny, *Man Belong Mrs Queen* is a great travel tale, and a fascinating account of an epic culture clash between the strange world of a British Prince Philip fan, and the even stranger world of a Prince Philip cult on a remote, beautiful South Sea island'
SIMON REEVE, author and BBC presenter

'With an appealing protagonist, a cast of vivid characters and a powerful sense of place, this is an excellent crime novel as well as a sharply observed slice of contemporary London life – and the good news is that it promises to be the first in a series.' GUARDIAN on *A Death at the Palace*

'A sparky, unexpected thriller . . . His delicate sense of place gives Baylis a special authenticity, which – when you add neat characterisation and plotting – make him a crime writer to watch.'
DAILY MAIL on *A Death at the Palace*

'M.H. Baylis introduces the London borough of Tottenham to crime fiction, and it performs extremely well . . . fast-moving, committed and very entertaining.'
THE TIMES on *A Death at the Palace*

'A richly enjoyable novel, working as both a satisfyingly plotted crime thriller, and a love letter to an often-overlooked corner of London.'
INDEPENDENT on *A Death at the Palace*

Man Belong Mrs Queen

Man Belong Mrs Queen

*Adventures
with the Philip Worshippers*

Matthew Baylis

First published in 2013 by Old Street Publishing Ltd,

Trebinshun House, Brecon LD3 7PX

www.oldstreetpublishing.co.uk

ISBN 978 1 908699 64 0

10 9 8 7 6 5 4 3 2

A CIP catalogue record for this title is available from the British Library.

Typeset by Martin Worthington

Printed and bound in Great Britain by CPI Group (UK) Ltd, Croydon, CR0 4YY

To my mother and father,
very much part of the journey.

Contents

Timeline

July – Aug 1774: Captain Cook visits Tanna, names the area 'New Hebrides'

July 1809: Russian explorer Golovnin visits Tanna

1825: Australian Peter Dillon lands on Tanna to buy sandalwood

1839: Williams and Harris, the first missionaries, arrive on Tanna

1842 Missionaries Turner and Nisbet land on Tanna

1843: Paddon and Towns establish first permanent white settlements in the New Hebrides

1849: Trader Leonard Cory sets up home on Tanna

1858: Missionary John G. Paton arrives on Tanna

1860s – 1904: Sandalwood trade, 'blackbirding' natives for the sugar plantations

1874-1877: Blackbirder Ross Lewin and trader Easterbrook murdered: British Navy sent to Tanna to intervene.

1885: First 'cargo cult' appears in Fiji

1896: Frank Paton, son of John G., establishes 'Tanna Law'

1904: 'White Australia' policy ends use of native labour – blackbirding comes to a close.

1907: Condominium government established - New Hebrides run jointly by France and Britain

1908, 1909: Tannese use British traders to appeal for government intervention against Tanna Law

1911: Mr Wilkes becomes District Agent on Tanna

1912, 1914: Wilkes gains important concessions for locals from the missionaries

1914: Emergence of the 'German Wislun' cult in nearby Papua New Guinea

1918: Wilkes replaced by Nichol

1921: Prince Philip born in Corfu

1922: Prince Philip leaves Corfu in an orange box

1939: Prince Philip meets the 13-year-old Princess Elizabeth

1940: First appearance of Jon Frum

1941: Tannese desert mission churches for Jon Frum dances

Dec. 1941: Japanese bomb Pearl Harbour – forcing USA to enter WWII

Jan 1942: Joe Nalpin's letter predicts Jon Frum will arrive by aeroplane. 29 Frumists sent to jail in Vila

May 1942: US aeroplanes duly appear – establishing military bases

Oct 1942: US troops sent to Tanna to suppress 'King' Neloyiag

1944: Nichol killed by his own truck

1945-50: Exiled Tannese spread Jon Frum to neighbouring islands of Ambrym, Malekula and Pentecost

1947: Frum supporters attack foreign owned stores; Prince Philip marries Princess Elizabeth

1951: Jake Navy and Captain World enter the Jon Frum pantheon

1952: British diplomat mistaken for Noah

1957: USS Yankee lands at Tanna to dispel cultic excitement

Deportees Allowed back; General Nakomaha's 'Tanna Army' march under the US flag.

All 650 of Tanna's Catholics join Jon Frum

1966: Mr Wilkes receives a pig from the elders of Yaohnanen, and doesn't give anything back.

1967: Emergence of the Nagriamel Independence movement on Santo

1971: Philip's first visit to the Pacific

Nagriamel leader Jimmy Stephens meets 'Phoenix' founder, the libertarian millionaire Michael Oliver

1973: Corsican Fornelli founds the 'Focona' kastom movement on Tanna

1974: Philip's second visit: sails past Tanna in the Royal Yacht Brittania

Fornelli raises the 'Focona' flag on Tanna, revolt suppressed

1976: funded by Phoenix, Jimmy Stephens petitions the UN in New York for support for independence

May 1977: Fornelli, 'King of Tanna', issues an ultimatum to HM Queen and President D'Estaing: get out!

September 1978: British officials present a signed photograph of Prince Philip to Yaohnanen

Jan 1980: Nation of Tafea declares independence – coinciding with revolt on Santo.

July 1980: New Hebrides becomes independent Vanuatu

CHAPTER ONE

Waiting for Something to Happen

PEOPLE on those islands dreaded the west wind, saying it was the wind that blew Pedro Fernández de Quirós, the first white man to reach their shores, four hundred summers before. At bedtime children still were chilled by their grandparents' tales of the floating houses, filled with pale ghosts, who killed men with their exploding sticks. When the wind blew, they sang special songs to chase it away.

A wind blew me into town, too – a gritty kind that came with blue skies and fast-moving clouds, more like the Mersey than Melanesia. 'Reminds me of home,' I murmured as I took my first steps on the island of Tanna. 'Yes, you will be broken in this place,' Nako said, pulling me from the path of a slow-moving luggage cart. It would turn out to be an apt pronouncement.

I'd picked up Nako, son of the chief of Yaohnanen village, in the capital, Port Vila, and we'd flown here with a crate of tools to build a school. That was part of the reason for my visit, anyway. I'd paid for Nako's flights, and the deal was that he'd be my guide and interpreter. It was a challenge to which he'd risen with grave enthusiasm, placing a blazer from Brisbane Girls' Grammar School over his trademark floral shirt. Nako, like many an enterprising Man Tanna, had been working as a taxi driver in Port Vila until some indistinct episode had relieved him of both vehicle and licence. He was now driving me instead.

In Lenakel, Tanna's main town, he had us wait several hours under a banyan tree, until a man with one tooth and a T-shirt bearing the legend 'Maximum Strength' gave us a ride in a truck. We drove down a sandy seaside road with nothing but churches on either side. Some were sturdy and log-built, seeming to frown upon the ramshackle tin tabernacles of their neighbours, whose wonky signs promised the imminent End of Time. One sign turned out to be a calendar of forthcoming attractions, and I was able to read it as our driver paused to let some goats cross the road. Monday: a talk by Pastor Peter Crean of the Church of the Alive and Descended Christ, Auckland. Tuesday: Ladies' Circle. Wednesday: ping-pong. If the end was nigh, then it wasn't as nigh as Wednesday. But it, and all the neighbouring signs and posters, told me something about the Tannese attitude to religion. It was their religions that interested me. And one in particular.

Just before the coastal road began to veer inland, we passed a group of Australian girls, coming screaming from the ocean in their bathing costumes. Nako said they were staying at the Lovely Bungalows. 'Two thousand five hundred vatu for every night.' For dark, tribal reasons beyond my ken, Nako possessed a number of crumpled brochures for the Lovely Bungalows in his kitbag, and one was now handed to our driver. I asked him why, but the only thing he'd say was that everything in his village, for a man like myself, would be free. Once I had acknowledged this with a gracious nod – it wasn't the first gracious nod I'd been required to give on the subject – he asked for several thousand vatu to pay for the truck.

Half an hour of chiefly vertical travel followed, up through folds of rain-fed palms to a village in the air. We dismounted in its nakamal, a huge circular meeting space outside the settlement. Nako cried 'Lhua!' in a high-pitched yodel and the surrounding bush turned, dream-like, into a crowd of approaching people: men and women, glistening from their work in the terraced yam gardens. Above us curled banyan trees like gnarled, paternal hands. Behind was Tukosmwera, tooth-like mountain home of gods. It was a dramatic setting. A circle formed around me. Everyone settled down for a good stare. Nako nipped off for a slash.

So this was the Man Ples: the people of the area. They were very black and covered in a film of dust that gave them the appearance of statues. The adults looked strong, and the children looked happy, but they all had great W's of grey snot on their upper lips, and rattling coughs. The men carried large machetes. What I mainly noticed, though, were the T-shirts.

Yaohnanen lies deep in 'kastom' territory. The word is Bislama pidgin, from the English word 'custom', and it means the old-school way of doing things. Traditional dress, meaning not much dress at all. Traditional ways, based on exchanging root vegetables and daughters with one's neighbours at periodic festivals. A dislike of money, a distrust of government, education, imported religion. Kastom also serves to separate certain groups of people from others. The political map shifts hourly, but at the point of my arrival, Yaohnanen's people were on cool terms with the Christians, who worshipped Christ, and the John Frum cult, who worshipped America. In Yaohnanen, the Duke of Edinburgh was the focus of religious devotion. And that was really why I'd come to Tanna.

Guidebooks to this kidney-shaped isle of eighteen thousand souls spoke of charming villages, whose near-naked inhabitants pursued Stone Age lifestyles with savage joy. They neglected to mention the chilly maritime winds, or the fact that, when not performing rituals, most kastom people made do with hand-me-down clothes from the missions and the NGOs. It was the T-shirt, rather than the grass skirt or the pandanus-leaf penis cover, that most Tannese reached for in the mornings.

MATTHEW BAYLIS

And judging by the extensive exhibition of T-shirts
I viewed during those first few hours, the folk of
Yaohnanen worshipped a number of things besides
Prince Philip. Manchester United had a vigorous cult
going there – as did Irish teen pop combo BoyZone
and the Holy Trinity of Japanese electronics manufac-
turers. I'd been told by anthropologists who'd worked
in the region that it was wrong to think of the Tannese
as being some obscure community on the edge of the
world. And they were right. Every sunrise, I thought,
must bring some representative from ICI, Fox Studios
or the Ford Motor Company, keen to hook the locals
into some lucrative sponsorship deal.

A small girl with a hazy afro of spun gold presented
me with a bunch of wild mandarins. It felt rude to scoff
them before this attentive audience, so I offered them
around. Everyone laughed. A chunky fellow clapped
me on the back and pointed to the trees around the
edge of the meeting ground. Their branches hung low
with mandarins.

Under intense scrutiny I unzipped one of my bags
and withdrew two packages. The first contained lollipops, for the kids. The second contained short,
white clay pipes, an essential style accessory for the
kastom-conscious dude. I offered one to the man
who'd pointed at the trees. He tried to look pleased,
at which point I realised I'd offered him a lollipop. I
had another go.

There ensued a scene like the opening moments of Harrods' sale, with men and children clambering over one another in their rush to inspect my wares. A pipe was shattered. A toddler had his lolly snatched from his hands and set up a howl. My new friend took the last remaining pipe – there was a whiff of the demi-monde about this individual, who'd eschewed the traditional T-shirt/shorts combo in favour of a lady's handbag and the top half of a lemon-coloured safari suit. I saw he was holding the longest pipe – a slightly more ornate affair with the detail of a hand holding the bowl. He patted my hand appreciatively. I wasn't surprised – I'd meant to give that one to the Chief. Some of the others seemed to realise this, or at least, to share the view that the pipe ought to go somewhere else. Bickering broke out.

Nako, emerging from the bush, shot me a look containing awe as well as annoyance. It took a certain kind of anthropological genius, he seemed to imply, to get a group of people at war with itself in three minutes. I recalled Prince Philip asking that aboriginal elder if they still chucked spears at one another. Give me time, I thought, and I could outgaffe the Duke of Gaffes.

There was a shout from the path that led into the village. Tough little lop-sided Nako stiffened. A thin-limbed old man paced towards us. Dressed in a grey tracksuit top and a faded sarong, he held the hem of the lower garment delicately as he walked, like a Buddhist monk. The villagers stilled. I guessed this was Chief Jack Naiva, last surviving founder of the Prince Philip cult. He glanced at his son Nako and spoke some words to him in the local language.

I couldn't catch what this old man had said, but it seemed a dry, loveless encounter. I knew Nako was about forty, and had spent some years away from the island. On our shopping trips together in Port Vila, I'd prised out of my guide the information that he sometimes missed his village, and was pleased to be going home. But Nako didn't look pleased now.

Chief Jack padded closer and the crowd parted. I could see from the way he peered at me that his eyes – ringed with beautiful long lashes – were no longer strong. He gave me a gruff nod, glanced towards the bubble wrap at my feet and made a pronouncement. Within moments every pipe that had been taken up was gently replaced in the bag. Safari Suit gave a shrug, as if to say, 'Well, it was worth a go,' before handing back his booty. Somehow he managed to snap the thing in two along the way, earning himself a shrivelling look from the Chief.

When all the other pipes were back at my feet, Chief Jack squatted down, and motioned to me to do the same. He gave me the sort of long, piercing look that suggested he was downloading the contents of my soul for later perusal, and then spoke directly to me in the local tongue. Once again, it was beyond me, and it was a very long speech. When he'd finished, all the men slapped their shins.

'He says "Hello,"' Nako translated, squatting at my side.

'Was that it?'

Nako rolled his eyes. 'He will raise a big meeting, a big tok-tok, for the Big Men, and the pipes from Philip will be passed into the hands of the Man Ples.'

'They're not Philip's pipes, they're...'

'And he says that he had a dream of you.'

'A dream?' I'd heard Tanna was a market garden of religious movements, its seers seeking inspiration in dreams and drug-induced reveries. 'Can I ask him what the dream was?'

'No.'

The Chief took my hand. His felt like leaves – cool and dry. And then he spoke in Bislama, the English-based pidgin that helps the people of the Vanuatu archipelago, with their eighty islands and their 118 languages, understand one another. 'Bilip,' he said. 'Me wantem come.'

Philip. I want him to come.

It sounded aggrieved, as if Philip, Duke of Edinburgh, King of the World and son of the local mountain god, was pushing it a bit and the Chief had had enough. Then he tapped the ground and pointed at me. What brought you here? 'Long story,' I said. They understood, because the words mean the same in Bislama. And they laughed at that, and settled down around us on logs and stones, in that windy, dusty meeting ground, rubbing their hands. Down Tanna way, they love a long story.

It was 1982 when Prince Philip rode in a train to Manchester, passing right by my bedroom window, and waved at me.

A little of the above is true. The Duke of Edinburgh certainly went to Manchester, to deliver a speech at Salford University. There was a train line to Manchester that went past my bedroom window, too, but Philip travelling on a train and waving out of it at me was just a family joke, something my parents said in the weeks before the royal visit, probably because they couldn't imagine anything more ridiculous than Prince Philip being friendly to us.

It caught my eleven-year-old imagination, though. There were shades of *The Railway Children* in the idea, of the mysterious stranger who changes the children's lives merely by clattering by on the 8.15 to Charing Cross and waving; the wider, childhood fantasy of greatness singling you out with its twiggy finger.

For that reason, rather than any precocious interest in global politics, I found myself following what happened on that trip of Philip's to Salford University. It was there, during his Vice-Chancellor's address, that he said one of the downsides of eradicating disease and hunger was more disease and hunger.

I thought it made some sense. Drugs lower immune systems. Rising populations lead to epidemics and food shortages. My form teacher – who'd been nurturing in me an interest in anthropology by loaning me books containing pictures of bare-breasted tribeswomen – confirmed this. It was a point, he said, so old hat among population experts that nobody even debated it any more. For everyone else, though, it represented Prince Philip's personal attack upon the poor and the hungry. I noticed nobody was really interested in discussing what Philip said. They just seemed to enjoy being angry about it.

My mum, a keen observer of matters monarchy-related, said it had always been so. Long before my birth, Prince Philip had been spotted by Enoch Powell, making faces in the gallery of the House of Commons. Politicians on both sides of the House had then united, briefly, in telling the Duke to get lost. They'd called him a 'useless reactionary arrogant parasite', she told me, the 'most well-paid social security claimant in Britain'. The Speaker had even had to order them to tone down their language. So Philip was damned for getting involved, damned for doing nothing.

Children are preoccupied with fairness, perhaps because they often feel short-changed by the adult world. I felt Philip wasn't getting a fair deal, and I felt it was sad that no one stuck up for him. Moving on from that position, I became curious about the personality that made so many so very angry. My interest in him, in itself, seemed to make such people even angrier, and some prickly part of me decided, in turn, that this was quite fun.

This was 1982, the year after Prince Charles married Diana Spencer, and there was still a backwash of monarchy-related cargo swilling around the town's charity shops and jumble sales. Before long, I'd kitted out my room with a Prince Philip poster, a dozen cellophane flags and a fine collection of illustrated books. It was in perusing the more detailed of these that I discovered Philip to be far from the figure he was widely thought to be. 'Phil the Greek' wasn't Greek. He was posh, certainly, but he'd experienced a bleak childhood, shunted between his eccentric European relatives, who included Nazis and friends of Freud. His mother had turned into a mystic, his dad bequeathed him a suit and razor before dying in the arms of his mistress. But no one ever mentioned these things.

I started to think we'd be friends. I was the kind of boy whose classmates convulsed with laughter whenever he spoke up. I knew why, because I'd inherited from my parents a certain curious, old-fashioned way of speaking, and using words from books, and it set me apart, set all of us apart as a family, from most of the people in the town where we lived. 'We seek to purchase,' my father once informed a Dixon's sales assistant, as he accompanied me on an end-of-summer pencil-case-replenishing

trip, 'a calculator of which robustity is a salient feature.'
What can you do when you're living in Southport, Mer-
seyside, and it's 1982, and your dad talks like that?

My brother went blissfully the other way, acquiring a
fishtail parka and such a ferociously strong local accent
that even the locals had trouble understanding him.
I dug my heels in, though, and looked for a standard
to carry into battle, and it was the Duke of Edinburgh.
Unpopular, posh, misunderstood and mocked, like
me. I wrote to him. He didn't reply. I wrote to *Jim'll Fix
It*, too, and they did write back. But they said fixing that
sort of thing – tea in the Palace with the Duke – was
beyond them. But I didn't care. We didn't really need
to meet. We shared a bond, brothers in obscurity.

Over time, adolescent self-absorption guaranteed I
had less time for Duke worship. I changed schools, and
some sensible part of me realised that one could not
be a card-carrying Prince Philip fan at a Northern boys'
school in the eighties and hope to live. The royal posters came down, and were replaced by images of Lenin
and mushroom clouds, both of which you could purchase in Woolworth's at the time.

But the eighties to the mid-nineties was a golden age
for the Duke of Edinburgh, a period during which he
racked up, among others, the Chinese (slitty eyes), the
Hungarians (pot bellies), the Solomon Islanders (out
of their minds) and the Scots (drink-driving/alcohol-
ics) as sworn enemies. With the rest of the population,

I experienced a certain delicious outrage at his comments. I realised we all rather looked forward to hearing news of his latest public pratfall, decidedly more than we did to royal nuptials or the endless births of their offspring or their trips to Spalding to open spinal injuries units.

Then one day, as I sat in a draughty East Anglian lecture hall, something reawoke my love affair with this unlovable duke. We undergraduate anthropologists were watching a BBC film made on Tanna that told the remarkable story of the John Frum cult, and one of the interviewees was a sharp-eyed, bony individual with red feathers in his hair. This man – I'd later discover he was Tuk Noao, a legendary Tannese philosopher-speech-maker – spoke of how his body contained a white man and a black man, happily co-existing. He kept a special hut with a typewriter and a chair to cater to his European side. And behind him, throughout the interview, yet never mentioned or highlighted, was a signed photograph of Prince Philip.

At the end of the film I asked the lecturer about the photograph. And she gave an embarrassed giggle and said, 'Yes, they've got a bit of a Prince Philip cult going there.' The idea of Prince Philip, widely regarded as a racist buffoon, being worshipped on this far-flung island of black men, proved so intriguing that I couldn't leave it at that. What circumstances had caused this man of Tanna to have a signed picture of

Philip in his hut? How did it fit into his idea of white and black united in the one body? My lecturer became evasive – I think she just wanted her lunch – but she suggested a couple of books. And they told me even less. It was one cult, in an area full of them. Its members held the Duke of Edinburgh in special regard. End of story.

Over the remainder of that year I asked all the other anthropology staff what they could tell me. Like the first one, they became shifty. They'd try to divert my attention towards safer territory: the pangolin cult of the Lele tribe, the insulting oral poetry bouts of the Inuit. My tutor even said to me, in that feverish month before my finals, 'You have to stop mentioning this Prince Philip stuff in every essay. You won't get any marks for it. And why are you so obsessed?'

I couldn't really answer him, at least not when I had to memorise an article entitled 'Symbolic Hair' before Wednesday. But it was a fair question. A perverse, geeky preoccupation, I suppose, with discovering the truth behind what passed as truth. The same contrariness, the same irascible quality that led me once to tack Prince Philip posters to my bedroom walls, fired me up about this cult of his. It wasn't enough just to know it was there. Why was it there? What did it do for the people who'd invented it?

There were newspaper articles from time to time, most of them calling it an offshoot of the John Frum,

America-worshipping affair on the other side of Tanna, and always identifying it as a 'cargo cult'. Like a score of other native movements that had unsettled the Pacific region since the 1880s, the islanders were said to be waiting for some huge shipment of fridges, guns, trucks and washing machines to appear over the horizon. They didn't understand money and shops, they just coveted the white man's goods (usually alongside wanting the white man to bugger off home) and thought they could get them through some messianic version of *Sale of the Century*, compered by the Duke of Edinburgh. Even the Royal Family's website described it pretty much that way.

And there was nothing that went further, nothing asking why. The accepted view, however politely expressed, was that the Tannese were just barking mad. Obscure, mud-bespattered tribesmen, deluded by their home-grown drugs, oblivious to the mocking cries of the world, just waiting for princes and white goods to fall from the sky. It struck me that we wouldn't show such a lack of curiosity about any other group of people. No other faith or native movement on the face of the earth, however bizarre its claims, would warrant such stark indifference.

I wrote to Prince Philip twice again, once receiving a brush-off from his secretary, once a packet of archive material relating to the time the Royal Family first became aware of the cult, in 1978. It told me that some people on Tanna believed Philip to be the son of the god who inhabited their local mountain. He'd gone away, but would return, and when he did, miracles would occur. But this account was still full of question marks.

It did, however, make me realise that Prince Philip knew even less about the cult than me. And it struck me as sad that he'd never been to the island. He'd travelled the world in his yacht, I'd come to understand that the South Pacific occupied a special place in his heart – and I did believe he had one – yet the village where they worshipped him, the one place where this unpopular figure was loved, lay behind an invisible cordon of protocol. Poor Philip, condemned to open rural health centres and pumping stations, stand stiffly to the anthems of nations whose very names make his eyelids droop, to be Queen's Consort, never King, and yet to have a kingdom he could never see. What the Prince needed was an Anthropologist Royal, someone who could go to Tanna and root out the truths he could not.

Trying to please some distant father figure – that's how a Freudian analyst friend described my mission. My dad enjoyed the sort of 1930s boyhood that rather terrified me when I read about it in books: forever scrumping apples, rigging up wirelesses from discarded rubbish, foraging for bits of shot-down aeroplanes. It pained him to see me lounging on the sofa or drifting through rooms in a trance. I sometimes asked my dad why the mere sight of me made him so cross. 'You just look like you're waiting for something to happen!' he bristled.

Waiting for something to happen. And it was that phrase that boomed in my head, like gong, bell and monk's mantra, when I first learned about the Philippists. Here were people whose whole religious outlook was built upon waiting. Waiting for Prince Philip to return to Tanna, waiting for his arrival to usher in a utopia. Waiting year after year for events which, logic and reason and facts dictated, would never ever happen. As I sat in front of the Chief, my father's words came back on the sea-wind. I'd been waiting for something to happen, too. It was this.

A crowd of expectant tribal faces gathered around me in the meeting–place, most of them now chomping on lollipops. A chilly wind had started to blow through the trees, and the man in the safari suit helpfully set light to a heap of damp leaves just right of my elbow. 'Fire,' he said – as if I might be in doubt. Which I could have been, because the arrangement did nothing except waft yellow, choking smoke into my face. Overcoming a paroxysm of coughing, I got up and moved. Wrinkled with concern, my new friend simply kicked the fire to one side, so I was still within its suffocating orbit.

'Can I ask more questions now?' I croaked at Nako.

'Oh yes,' he said solemnly. 'Here you will get the special knowledge of the Prince Philip.' Nako spoke a form of English that was not so much broken, as decoratively bruised. But I'd be relying on it heavily over the coming weeks. With everyone else, I'd be required to speak pidgin, or fall back on the two hundred-odd words of the local tongue I'd memorised before I flew out.

'Right, excellent. I want to know when...' Something about doing anthropology, even as an amateur, obliges you to talk in a firm, British-Consul-taking-no-nonsense voice, like Ronald Coleman seeing off a horde of Pathans. '...when you first knew about Prince Philip.'

The Chief's eyes widened in horror.

'You cannot ask that,' Nako said.

'Erm. OK. Why not?'

Nako seemed about to add something, but he was interrupted.

'We have always known him,' Chief Jack replied, in a quavering, slightly indignant voice. 'We knew him in *Wolwatu.*'

World War Two. 'That was when you first learned about Prince Philip?' It didn't fit with what I'd understood previously, but it was possible. Perhaps some Tanna lads, assisting with the American war effort in Port Vila, could have picked up the odd news report of Prince Philip's distinguished naval career. Mentioned in dispatches for his deft use of the searchlight during the Battle of Matapan. A naval legend, for his cunning ruse off the coast of Sicily, when he diverted enemy shells away from HMS *Wallace* by attaching a flaming raft to the back of the ship. An all-action chap, Philip, the very kind they admired on Tanna.

'No,' Chief Jack replied firmly. 'Maybe some people like Kowiya, down in Yakel, took the truth then. But it has always been ours.' Sitting next to him, Nako nodded. They made an odd pair: the lean, ascetic holy man and his son, who looked like the sort of sailor destined to spend his shore leave in a prison cell. 'It was ours, and we knew he was our god from before everything. But it is better not to talk about it.'

'Why do you say Philip is your god?'

Chief Jack embarked upon a long answer, but I didn't grasp much of it. I'd gone to extreme lengths to find a lexicon of the local language, and boned up on this before leaving the UK, as well as learning Bislama. The Chief seemed to have his own version of both these tongues, however, and he mingled them at will. I did catch a few words here and there. *Captain Cook. Mr Wilkes and Mr Wilkie. America.* All of them little beacons in the stormy history of Tanna's contact with white men. But pointing where?

Perhaps, I thought, we should begin with more concrete matters – tabernacles, sacred sites and forms of worship. 'Can I see the place where you worship him?' I asked. 'Is there a place?'

'You will see everything,' Chief Jack assured me. 'Nako has brought you to the place.' He gave his son a curt nod, and the effect of it was to relax him considerably. My guide wasn't given to overt displays of bonhomie, at least not with me, but now Nako patted me on the back in a chummy way.

'My father will show everything now.'

'Great,' I said, springing to my feet and going over to my bags. I would need my cameras for this. On the series of long flights around the globe, I'd had no need for the movies or the on-tap music, but been swathed delectably in dreams of what I'd discover on the smoky slopes of Tanna. Bamboo tabernacles filled with royal mugs and Jubilee cake tins, Union Jacks guarded by spear-wielding tribesmen, a miniature Buckingham Palace on stilts. But I'd never imagined it would be so easy.

'What are you doing?' Nako called over. I glanced up. Everyone was still seated, staring at me with the sort of bug-eyed affrontedness you receive if your mobile phone goes off at the opera.

'I'm just getting my...' my voice trailed away. 'I thought we were going to look at...'

'Not *now*,' Chief Jack said. He shook his head, appalled at my carryings-on. 'Now it is time for kava.'

I sat back down to a chorus of rolled eyes and quiet tutting. Rather like English country ladies responding to a queue jumper in the garden centre, they weren't about to say I'd committed an offence, but they were certainly going to let me know. Men began to fetch long, green kava roots from the gardens just behind, while the women were shooed away so that the real business could begin. The wind picked up some more and the boys brought firewood.

The man in the safari suit introduced himself as Siyaka. He had the wide, agreeable face of a teddy bear, a clipped beard and a dead bird in his pocket. He showed the bird to me. I wasn't quite sure what reaction was expected, but I knew the word for bird in the Kwamera language, so I thought I'd impress him.

Siyaka screamed. He called his mates over and told me to repeat what I'd just said.

'Why are you speaking Kwamera?' asked a silver-haired gentleman in a vest celebrating Iron Maiden's 1987 tour of the Benelux countries.

'I learnt some before I came here,' I declared proudly, 'so that we could understand one another better.'

'We don't speak Kwamera,' Siyaka said joyously. 'We speak Nauvhal.'

This was troubling. But Tanna, an island just eighteen kilometres in length, had six of its own languages. It struck me that, in a place so small, the tongues ought to be mutually intelligible.

'We can understand it,' Siyaka conceded. 'But we don't like it much.'

'*Bleh bleh bleh,*' added the man in the vest. 'See? Not like our language.'

So I'd spent three months learning a complex language that was not only not spoken in the Yaohnanen area, but actively disapproved of. I trusted this would be the last major error. I was wrong to.

'Most white men come to stay with old Chief Kowiya,' Siyaka said, stuffing the bird back into his pocket. Its leg remained poking out at a wild angle, like a ghastly lapel badge.

'Well, actually, I've got to....'

I was distracted as the bird began to seep some morbid discharge across the front of Siyaka's jacket. 'Maybe Kowiya used magic,' Siyaka said, 'to make you learn the wrong language, so you'd have to stay with him.'

'Does Chief Kowiya speak Kwamera then?'

'No. Anyway, what's up there is stronger than anything Kowiya's got.' Siyaka pointed to the jagged mountain behind him and winked.

At this point, Nako told me the kava was ready, urging me to cross the floor of the meeting place with him. I did as I was bidden, but not with a light heart. Tanna's kava had a formidable reputation throughout Melanesia – there were fourteen varieties on the island, some of them so strong they could turn you into a flying fox. Or at least make you believe this. And I did, to be frank, nurture the odd reservation about taking a hitherto-untried narcotic in a mountain village many thousands of miles from home, surrounded by machete-wielding cultists.

As it turned out, the kava wasn't ready, but Nako led me over to watch the production line, where my insight into the preparation process gave me additional cause for concern. On some islands, and in the commercial kava bars of Port Vila, the fibrous root was milled in a mincing machine, then mixed with rain water. The men of Tanna viewed this approach in much the way that connoisseurs of Château Lafite might view the manufacture of fizzy Lambrusco. Their kava was carefully scrubbed with coconut fibre to remove the harmful alkaloids, hacked into chunks and then chewed by virgin boys. The resultant mixture of saliva, mud and fibre was strained through a mesh, mixed with water from a petrol can and then drunk straight from a coconut shell.

I realised, while watching the preparations, how very much the people must value the end product. No society, for sure, would sink that amount of labour into a bowl of muddy boy-spit, if it didn't get them most regally fuck-faced. It was more serious than that, though. The women were banished from the area while the work went on, forbidden, Nako told me, to even look at the roots, let alone taste of their bounty. In the past, he said, a touch wistfully, any woman who broke the taboo was buried up to her neck in the earth. Nowadays the women scooted around the sides of the nakamal on thickly screened paths – the only penalty for incursion, if the blokes were so inclined, being a quick biff on the head with a kava plant. And the men, too, had their privations to observe. Virgin boys could handle the product at will, but a married man must take great care not to touch the masticated mass of kava pulp, for fear of losing his sexual and physical powers.

The Chief now urged me to drink. Each Tannese village, I knew, possessed a stock of important ritual and political titles, handed out to boys and girls in infancy. You took your kava according to your place in this often rather fluid hierarchy, but, as a great courtesy, I was waved forward for the first slug. I had, in fact, approached fist-fights in pub toilets, picked up girlfriends from abortion clinics, with greater enthusiasm than I felt at that moment. Across the floor of the meeting place, Siyaka flashed me another wink.

I glanced back at Mount Tukosmwera, wondering what Siyaka's earlier comment had meant, then was directed to swallow the contents of the shell in one gulp. My throat had different ideas, though, and caused me to spray a liberal portion over the ground and the feet of the men standing closest to me. Everyone nodded approvingly. I had made an excellent tamafa, Nako said, in a low voice.

'Thanksh,' I replied carefully. The kava – a distant relative of the pepper plant – tasted of medicated clay, not unlike that stuff that dentists like to fill your mouth with before starting a conversation with you. It numbed everything in its path, lips, tongue, throat, oesophagus and finally the entirety of my being. A fierce-looking man, all muscles and moustache in a tight Wallabies singlet, handed me something like a warm piece of moon rock.

'Wassit?' I asked blearily.

'Nuhunu,' he answered gruffly.

Staring at the object in my hand, I dimly recalled having heard the word before. Kirk Huffman, an anthropologist with decades of experience in the area, had kindly briefed me when I'd passed through Sydney. A sprite-like presence, with dapper suits and a conquistador beard, he'd given me a crash course in Tannese etiquette in the coffee bar of a museum. 'The nuhunu's a little bit of cooked food – you eat it straight after the kava. Means you get some dinner inside you before your appetite goes.'

I sniffed at the piece of moon rock and found it to be vaguely like a potato. I took a mouthful, but was unable to swallow it. I wandered to the edge of the bush to spit it out unseen. The fierce-looking man joined me there – he reminded me of a former PE teacher – and let out a string of terrifying howls and whoops into the undergrowth. Eventually these echoed back, but in different form, as if further PE teachers in distant valleys were simultaneously comparing scores for the high jump. I turned round. Some sizeable stretch of time seemed to have gone by without my realising it. A silent awards ceremony was taking place in the nakamal – each man being called up to take his shell, more kava being strained and decanted, and the whole thing conducted in whispers as the sun slowly faded away. I felt as if we were all suspended in glue.

'Everybody is quiet in the nakamal,' Siyaka hissed. 'No speak.' He promptly stubbed his toe on a jagged log and swore loudly. When someone lobbed a stick at him, he dropped his voice. 'Everybody listen to the kava.'

Rubbing his injured toe with one hand, he pointed to his kinsmen, like an exhibition of statues in stock-still poses around the meeting place. Some sat in pairs or threes, some alone. How could they be so calm? I wondered. The kava was writhing in my ribcage now, like a gecko with a rash. I wanted to bellow, to hop from foot to foot, tear off my clothes and swoop down through the trees to the crashing sea.

And then, just as suddenly, I wanted to do none of the above. It wasn't that I couldn't move, or speak, so much as that I'd lost all desire to. If I did anything – scratched my ear, or flexed my jaw – I found that, seconds later, I'd frozen in the act, lost upon a wind of thoughts so loud, so clear they seemed to come from outside myself. I was listening, I guessed, to the kava.

And it asked me what I knew. What I hoped to know before I went away again. I knew there'd been a dispute here on Tanna, when a visiting official forgot to recipro-cate a gift. That was in 1966, the same year Prince Philip said British women didn't know how to cook. And while the ladies of the UK were being outraged, the elders of one small Tannese village made their own wounded feelings known in a series of cryptic pronouncements. They referred to a broken clay pipe, and asked when it would be mended. They said they wanted something from the white man's world, but which belonged to them. The British government took eleven years to work out what they were on about. And then it made amends, in a most surprising way.

I glanced around the darkening space. Nothing but trees and rocks and logs. So did they really do any worshipping here? Did they, as other Melanesian cultists had done, march in military formation or speak on 'telephones' made of creeper vines to summon the Prince and his cargo. What was the cargo, anyway – simple stuff like axes and bush knives? Laptops and trucks to put them on a par with Western whites? Or tanks and guns to chase them into the sea?

Captain Cook. Mr Wilkes and Mr Wilkie. America.

I sensed something vital in the Chief's answer. It didn't seem a coincidence that I'd brought with me several history books, to study whenever I wasn't asking questions. The kastom men lived long, but their memories were longer, and the roots of the cult of Prince Philip would surely trail right back to the first instances of contact between black and white. I would be looking there, just as I would be looking in the reed huts and the smoky nakamals of the present. I prayed the wind blowing now was not a westerly. That it was a kind one,

one that would send me to the right places, without the fear that met the first white faces on Tanna's shores.

'Me likem you,' hissed an urgent voice among the trees. It was the big, awkward man, Siyaka. And I liked him too – not least because he broke things and bumped into things and was always being shouted at by everyone else. I said so, in a roundabout way, and he slapped me on the back, a move that left me gasping for breath.

'Perhaps you are the other half of me,' he said, explaining that all Tanna men had a doppelganger, sometimes on the other side of the earth, whose strength and brain power they could dip into by spiritual means. That was why they were so strong, why the Americans had wanted to recruit them, above all other islanders, during the war. It was why Tanna men and white men had a secret bond. 'Why are you smiling?' he asked.

'I've just started work.'

CHAPTER TWO

Ken Dodd, the Invisible Jungle Orchestra and a Mysterious Case of Myth Stealing

I DREAMT of a woodpecker drilling at the log bed I slept upon, and then, as sunlight streamed in cheese-grater formations through the cane walls, I swam upwards to the day. There was a tapping sound, it seemed, but nothing to do with birds. The entire hut was shaking. The underside of the roof, made from reeds, swayed sexily from side to side like a dancer in a rah-rah skirt; I watched, agog, as a nail popped out of the wall. Placing my feet upon the packed-earth floor, I discovered that, too, to be quivering like a cold dog.

I raced from the hut, shouting 'Earthquake!' at the top of my voice. The door in the adjacent hut flung open and an angry, bullet-shaped head shot out.

I'd stumbled home on dark bush ways from the first night's kava bout, my passage lighted by a smoulder-ing branch, and spent the night in a little enclosure

some yards from the village. It was reached by crossing a narrow creek, and up a small hill in the green-
ery behind it was a water tap. There was a reed hut for
Nako and myself, and next door to it, a very small structure, suitable, so I'd concluded in the drug-suffused
darkness of the night, for the storage of a few garden
tools.

The next morning, in the aftermath of the mini-
earthquake, I discovered that the small box contained
the PE teacher, who was called Kal, a younger brother
of Nako. 'Wanem?' he demanded curtly. What?

His head was joined at the doorway by the heads of
a small girl with a golden afro and a tubby boy about
three years old, and lastly by the belly of the most pregnant woman I had ever beheld. This family, cohabiting
in the sort of space we would set aside for our vacuum
cleaners, fixed me as one with an aggrieved frown.

'The earth was shaking!' I insisted. 'The trees! Everything!'

'The volcano,' Kal said witheringly.

'You're silly,' opined the small girl – at least, that
was the tone of it – and they all went back inside. I
remained where I was, sheepish, swathed in mist. I'd
heard about Mount Yasur, the island's active volcano – a central symbol in the beliefs of the John Frum
people. They believed the crater contained American
troops and trucks. Mount Yasur's ash, spewed from its
heart and blown continuously across the island, was the

reason Tanna's soil was so fertile, the reason no one had much work to do, and had so much spare time for thinking up new religions. And small wonder they were a religious lot, if the very soil they trod went into a spin cycle once a week.

Had Nako been in my hut, he could have told me not to make such a fuss. But only a telltale pebbledash of charred tobacco and spit revealed the recent presence of the man. I did some vague limbering exercises in the chilly air, reflecting that I needed some sort of absorbent mat to sleep on. This, in turn, caused me to muse upon the many other items I needed – a water bottle, a good torch, a diarrhoea remedy... Judging by the amount of water dripping off every bush and tree around me, a cagoule might have been a good idea, too.

And I'd had that good idea. Along with other good ideas concerning can openers, jumpers, extra blankets and the like – all of which had been duly purchased at a Chinese emporium in Port Vila bearing the name SELL ALL KIND GOOD. This cargo of good things was, as I stood shivering on the slopes of a Tannese mountain, languishing in the basement of a Port Vila motel. I hadn't packed it.

I now gazed at the reason I hadn't packed it: a large crate containing long nails, hammers and saws, stashed under the eaves of our hut. Anyone going to spend time in a kastom village had to make a useful gift to the community, and the deal I'd struck with Nako was that I'd provide tools for the construction of a schoolhouse.

They'd had a school before – encouraged by *National Geographic* photographer Karl Müller in the seventies. A hardened hell-raiser, an expert scuba-diver, beloved by women of all hues – Müller was revered on Tanna because he went around with few clothes on and knew how to kill a pig. Chief Jack Naiva was so impressed he named one of his sons after him – the bristling PE teacher next door. But even if Müller sounded like a rootin'-shootin' cliché of the travel world, he remained a figure to admire. His was a genuine passion for the traditional way of life, a genuine contempt for the way it had been eroded.

Karl Müller impressed on Chief Jack and the other notables of south-west Tanna that a kastom school would be a first-class way to keep their culture afloat. It would provide education for local boys, and follow a semi-tribal timetable: English in the morning, Myths in the afternoons. The school uniform was a nambas – a cover for the penis made of a dried, palm-like pandanus leaf and secured in place by a belt around the waist. The teachers would be paid in local produce, so as to avoid anything to do with the money economy. They accepted financial assistance from the British High Commission, but only on condition that the school was genuinely their own. They could even burn it down if they wanted.

They did in the end, but it lasted from 1976 to 1990, in spite of a troubled history. In the early years there was a lot of bother when the teachers tried to introduce desks and chairs, and they were reluctant to admit even a filing cabinet into the building. Many parents were alarmed by the whole idea of school – 'skul' was also the Bislama word for 'church', because in the past education had come always and only as a side order to missionary meddling. There was a further crisis in 1979, when it was rumoured the school was preventing the return of Prince Philip, and people in Yaohnanen kept their boys away. Eventually, local politics was its downfall and it dwindled away to naught.

I liked the idea of rebuilding the school, especially as girls were to be allowed to attend the new version, so Nako and I went on a major shopping expedition in Port Vila. I discovered, at the end of this, that we had acquired some 20 kilos of hardware, whereas the permitted maximum weight for all our luggage was far lower. There had, incidentally, been a side process whereby the list of necessary supplies had expanded to include various items that weren't even coming with us. There were some snazzy new deck shoes for Nako, a mighty drum of oil, and, least useful of all, in my limited, Western worldview anyway, a blue plastic wastepaper basket. I agreed to it all, though, anxious not to seem like some tight-fisted, suspicious white man, and reminding myself that I was going to be living as a guest of Nako's village. I also wanted some of its most precious commodity.

The islands in this part of Melanesia boasted a sophisticated system of copyright, whereby different groups jealously guarded their myths, songs, dances, techniques for making mats and war clubs, and weather-magic. They could be copied, but only with prior agreement. The slit drum, for example, a carved wooden gong used to summon people from the gardens to the meeting place, and as ubiquitous a symbol throughout Vanuatu as McDonald's golden arches back home, was originally the copyrighted design of Malekula island. But the Catholic missionaries, who invited themselves there in the nineteenth century, opposed kastom, going so far as to site their rubbish dump on top of an ancient burial ground. Fearing the demise of his traditions, Man Malekula smuggled the slit drum out, under cover of darkness, to nearby Ambrym. But men there copied the design and, in time, the classic version of the drum spread throughout the archipelago, though it was now synonymous with Ambrym. A century and a half on, Malekula men still hinted darkly at the recompense they were owed for this crime.

Westerners had also fallen foul of the rules. When I met him in Sydney, my anthropologist friend Kirk Huffman had alluded to another of his guild who'd been fatally poisoned for the theft of knowledge. When he wrote *The Happy Isles of Oceania*, Paul Theroux committed a further breach while interviewing key figures in the John Frum movement. He'd been told he could ask questions, but not write anything down. Mr Theroux thought he'd outwitted the Frumists by keeping everything in his head and writing it all down later. But they knew. And they were not pleased. If any knowledge was going to come my way, I decided, then I wanted full reproduction rights.

So I coughed up every time Nako made a request. And when it came down to the excess luggage issue, I reasoned that turning up without a few provisions of my own was less of a problem than turning up without the means to build the school. Nako backed me up in this, reminding me that his village contained everything a man could possibly need. Relieved, I consigned the bulk of my personal items to the basement of the motel.

But I had little chance to get into a proper gnash about this now, as the old Chief padded with his measured, dainty stride across the creek, carrying a sooty yam for my breakfast. He seemed annoyed that Nako wasn't around, and I was reminded of the curt way he'd greeted his son the day before. I should come directly to his hut in the main village, he said, where he had many things to show me. 'See everything,' he concluded portentously.

Excitedly, I grabbed my bag and accompanied him back along the path towards the nakamal. Learning the wrong tribal language for the area had been quite a setback. But the Chief spoke Bislama well, as it turned out – unlike some of the older tribesmen, who didn't know any – though his meaning was obscured by a lack of teeth and a tendency to discuss events in the spiritual realm as if they were on the middle pages of the local newspaper. Even so, it was perfectly OK for communication between us. We walked together like old friends through a tunnel of chattering Tanna greens: from jade, through avocado, to khaki and myrtle.

'I like you. You are serious,' the Chief said. 'Like Austin. Do you know him? Man belong Norway. Stayed down the hill a few years ago.'

I guessed he was referring to Øystein Vigestad, a Norwegian anthropologist whose thesis I'd actually brought with me. He'd been on Tanna a quarter-century before me, in the turbulent run-up to independence. All visitors were remembered like this, memorised like king-lists, each foreigner adding status to the village they stayed in.

'Then we had an American. Nice man, but he was always telling us silly things. Do you know, he told me his wife went out every day to work in a store, because if she didn't, then they couldn't pay the woman who was looking after his children?'

'I think he was probably telling you the truth.' The Chief stared at me in wonder. 'People do it because of their careers.'

The Chief cocked his head. 'What is a career?'

'It's like...' I blew air out of my cheeks. 'It's like ... instead of just doing work in order to eat and have kerosene for your lanterns, you're trying to get somewhere in your life. Climb up.'

'Ah yes,' the Chief nodded sagely. 'We have a career.'

'Do you?'

'Yes – it goes up the side of the waterfall, but nobody can decide whose job it is to fix it. It should be Kowiya, of course, but he's too mean.'

'Ah.'

Perhaps fortunately for me, we had reached the village by now, and the Chief proudly cast his hand around the place. This nakamal, he explained, was a famous one – one of the original twelve built by the ancestor gods of the island. 'Between each,' he explained reverently, 'they put a road. And between each road, more roads to join them.' He spun his hand about elaborately in the still air, describing an arrangement more complex than the Tokyo underground. 'From every village, a road. To every village, a road. Between every village, a road. And in every village, also, many roads.' He peered at me closely, as if examining his own reflection in a muddy pool. 'You understand?'

I did my best to look impressed, but I didn't really understand. Of course there were roads between the villages. Why would there not be?

'Passing from and to every important place on this island, there is a road,' the Chief added, for good measure. 'Except up there.' He pointed towards Mount Tukosmwera. 'Kalbaben put no roads there.'

'But I thought Prince Philip rode away to find Kwin Lisbet on a white horse,' I said, referring to a classic myth, collected on the island by anthropologists. 'How could he do that if there wasn't a road?'

'Many roads are blocked,' the Chief carried on, disregarding my question. 'This is when problems happen on the island, because people ignore the roads. You see?'

I nodded, but the Chief shook his head, as if he wasn't sure I'd really got his meaning. 'They block the road,' he muttered sadly. I started to wonder if this was just some old man's obsession – if he'd been in England, perhaps he'd have exhibited the same cranky devotion to railway bridges or trams.

'When Nako comes, he will help to explain,' the Chief said. And a murky look swept across his devout face, like the shadow of a cloud on a mountain. 'Where is he?'

The Chief's sudden irritation reminded me of a comment Kirk Huffman made when I told him I was going to Tanna with Nako. He'd known him in the eighties, employed him as a fieldworker to assist visiting anthropologists, and on that subject noted only that the arrangement hadn't quite worked out. He'd also said something like, 'You're going to be Nako's ticket, are you?' And I'd replied that yes, I was paying for his airfare, but I got the impression that that hadn't been quite what he meant. Kirk wasn't a man given to being mysterious, but did, to the chagrin of his wife and all who needed him, suffer from an ability to do several things at once. That conversation itself had taken place as he gave a telephone interview to a Spanish radio station, and did the shopping. Within seconds he'd started a peculiar sort of tuneless humming, then embarked on a thrilling, if untimely, discussion of cannibalism in Europe.

I left Australia without ever discovering what Kirk had meant. But now, as I walked towards the village with the Chief, I sensed some history between the wand-like old seer of the mountains and his loud-shirt-sporting, battered-looking son. Was it that age-old set-up, I wondered, so beloved of the sixties playwright: the son who leaves the village for a better life and finds he can never comfortably return?

As Chief Jack fell silent, I realised the surrounding bush was full of music. Not the steady, electric throb of the crickets, but something else, like fairy pipes on the breeze. It lent the scene such an unreal, filmic quality – the pale visitor and the visionary chief in the misty bush – that I laughed out loud. The Chief looked at me quizzically.

'What's the noise?' I asked.

'Oh, that. The boys are with their grandfathers,' he said mysteriously. 'Come on.'

The music had a sprite-like quality, but it was clumsy, too, all over the place, discordant, like a junior band practice. Perhaps it *was* a junior band practice. I longed to ask, but couldn't work out if it would be rude to. For almost half a millennium, after all, people of my kind had been visiting these parts and being rude. And worse.

As an addict of atlases, picture books and the *Vanishing World* series on TV, to me it felt like confirmation from the heavens when the headmistress of my primary school made me vice-captain of 'Cook' house. My reign was a virtuous one, I think – but the Whitby-born explorer blotted his copybook when he sailed to Tanna on board the *Resolution* in 1774. For a start, he got the name wrong.

Captain Cook's first sight of the local people left him underwhelmed. They were 'the most ugly, ill-proportioned people [I] ever saw ... a very dark-coloured and rather diminutive race, with long heads, flat faces and monkey countenances'. When they arrived on Malekula, Cook and crew were mobbed by locals crying, 'Temar', their word for 'ancestor'. These visitors, arriving from no known quarter of the world, with their skin the colour of skeletons, must surely be the dear departed. But the first hint of bother was at Erromango, the island immediately north of Tanna. There, a host of welcoming tribesmen tried to pull Cook's boat ashore. Cook took aim at the chief, who'd actually been doing his best to hold the crowds back. There ended up being four fatalities and two oars lost. Cook decided not to land in person, but sent a four-pound cannonball instead, at speed.

They met a more dignified reception on Tanna, where the locals sailed close in canoes and threw coconuts. Cook offered some cloth in return. But then it got out of hand. As the locals tried to seize the ensign, the cannon fired again. The next day there were dense crowds of Man Tanna down on the shore, heavily armed but still sending out welcoming parties with yet more coconuts. One native offered to trade a war club, then made off with the payment before handing it over. This gave Cook the opportunity to display more of his firepower, this time without hurting anyone. The Tannese did not scatter now – 'on the contrary, they began to halloo and make sport of it. One fellow showed us his backside in a manner which plainly conveyed his meaning.'

Others might have stayed away after such a display, but Cook went ashore. He drew a line in the sand and told the watching crowds not to cross it. Things seemed to improve, aided by the good offices of an old man called Paowang, for whom Cook developed a great respect. The visitors were allowed to collect fresh water and firewood. However, they could not entice the locals to part with any pigs. They offered plenty of iron goods – axes, knives and saws, but these were sniffed at. Nor did anyone want them to explore inland. This infuriated the eminent German naturalist Georg Forster, who nonetheless achieved some research, going about the coastal parts with large wooden plant presses on his back. Some of the natives were observed blowing kisses at him, which led Cook's party to assume they were homosexuals. Perhaps the backside display had been some sort of abrupt invitation, they thought, rather than an insult. But they got to the bottom of the mystery. On Tanna, only women carried loads on their backs. Forster, with his long, flowing locks, had been taken for a slightly rough specimen of European ladyhood.

Things proceeded peacefully enough, though, with Paowang being invited on board for some food and returning an axe lost in the woods. Eager to find out the name of this lush green isle, Cook held up a handful of soil and asked what they called it. Assuming that he wanted their word for soil, they told him it was 'muk-tanna'. And so Tanna the place became, even though none of the peoples there recognised it by that name.

Then one day some local lads strayed over the line in the sand. Cook's sentry shot one dead – an action which appalled Forster. Cook himself said it was unnecessary. He and the ship's surgeon went to help the young man, but arrived just in time to see him die. The

Tannese, terrified now by these unpredictable ghosts, brought offerings of coconuts, amid much grieving and anxiety. Cook and his party departed without delay, after just two weeks. He left a name for the archipelago – New Hebrides – although he never said exactly why.

But Cook's visit was part of a wider pattern – the next piece provided by the Russian explorer Captain Vasili Mikhailovich Golovnin. When he arrived in 1809, Golovnin made friends with an old chief called Gunama, whom he invited on board the ship *Diana*. Gunama decided 'Diana' was Golovnin's name and nothing could convince him otherwise. Or maybe Gunama was just having a bit of fun. At one point he asked Golovnin if they had any women on board and 'learning that we had not, he laughed loudly and indicated, by various highly explicit and all-too-intelligible signs, that women are essential'. Gunama continued to make a joke out of this, asking Golovnin and his crew how they could perpetuate their race without women, and occasionally hunting for them on the ship.

Golovnin kept Cook's journals to hand throughout his trip, determined not to make the same mistakes. He laid down strict rules for his crew as to the goods they could barter, anxious for there to be no misunderstandings. He gathered local words to make communication easier. When people signalled that they didn't want the visitors to enter certain areas, they didn't push their luck.

Golovnin went to unusual lengths to make *Diana*'s stay a peaceful one. When Gunama took a shine to his brass-buttoned coat, the Russian was reluctant to disappoint him. So he had the ship's tailor knock up a bizarre costume – 'a hospital-style robe ... assorted ribbons sewn onto it ... and ... as many brass buttons, hooks and other trifles as possible ... sewn onto the garment'. Once Gunama saw Golovnin in this garb, he completely forgot about the naval jacket – and Golovnin was, of course, happy to hand over his technicolour dream coat. This move backfired slightly when it became apparent that Gunama was by no means the only chief on the island. Various aggrieved members of Tanna's aristocracy showed up, wondering where their coats were. Golovnin duly got the tailor working overtime. When the ship finally departed after six days, the visitors were given a tearful farewell. And a yam weighing sixteen and a half pounds. Not a shot had been fired.

The fact that Golovnin and his men received such a warm welcome on Tanna is due, in part, to his rare cultural sensitivity. But it also demonstrates that the Tannese had not forgotten the violence of Cook's visit, thirty-five years earlier. The Russians didn't need to fire their guns, because the Tannese now knew what guns could do. It was also significant that, apart from instilling the fear of firepower, Cook's party had made no visible cultural impact. Golovnin could find no European artefacts from Cook's era. The only suspect, an iron bolt, turned out to be something one of Golovnin's men had picked up at the Cape of Good Hope and was using to jam a door open. It seemed all traces of the marauding ghosts had been flung into the sea.

These opening steps in the dance of contact set up a pattern that would repeat itself many times throughout the next two hundred years. Different kinds of white men arrived on the shores of Tanna – some with cannon and musket, some with consideration and manners. If you are a stranger to the European and his ways, it can be tough to make sense of it all. And that's usually where religion helps.

Chief Jack stored the apparatus of his own religion in a rusty souvenir biscuit tin. He led me into a near-empty village, composed of squat reed huts in a circular pattern, and bade me sit on a simple bench outside his quarters. He disappeared inside, and shortly afterwards a roar was followed by a smacking sound, and that followed by the squeals of a piglet exiting the premises at high speed. The Chief himself then emerged, having exchanged the sportswear and sarong for the nambas. Now a proud man of kastom, he was ready to show me the secrets of his faith.

I was both amazed and disappointed by my first visit to Chief Jack's tabernacle. I'd been repeatedly promised that I would 'see everything', be shown all that I could need to know, and however hard I tried to remain dispassionate, this had given rise to visions of dark-fronded tabu houses and smoking altars. The mildewed contents of an old cream-cracker box couldn't quite compare.

Then again, there was still something pretty remarkable about this old man, in a Melanesian mountain village, proudly displaying a collection of newspaper clippings about the Royal Family. There were bits about Charles and his organic farm. Outrage over Prince Harry and his drunken antics in a Nazi uniform. And, of course, Philip: offending entire nations, presiding over unspeakably dull committees, bumping off his daughter-in-law…

'How do you get all this stuff?' I asked, switching on my voice recorder and balancing the microphone on the seat next to me.

'Friends all across the world send it. And Ken Dodd.'

'Sorry?'

'Ken Dodd.'

I tugged at my ear, wondering if some insect had set up home inside it while I slept. Or maybe this was the deadly undertow of last night's kava drinking. Perhaps I'd just misheard. He might have said Ken Todd. Or Kent Odd. He simply can't have meant Ken Dodd, the Mersey mirth-maker, buck-toothed King of the Diddymen. That was too weird, even for Tanna.

'I have his book inside,' the Chief went on. 'I will show you.'

He didn't, though, because at that instant a great joyous, sweaty work party filed through the village, the women loaded up with sugar canes and the men swinging their machetes about like flags. Among them was Kal, fierce as ever, fixing me with a policeman's stare. He murmured something in his father's ear, glaring at me all the while. In the meantime the villagers settled around us in an expectant, sooty huddle.

'He wants to know if you are happy to be on Tanna again,' Chief Jack said.

'Well … erm…' It was, coming from the perpetually scowling Kal, quite a pleasant overture, and I regretted being unable to return it with the full vigour it deserved. 'This is my first time,' I said.

'No, it isn't,' Chief Jack replied amiably. 'How did you know how to make the tamafa last night when you drank the kava?'

'The what?'

In the manner of someone telling me the best way to turn some four-by-two into a spice rack, the Chief explained that, when the sun went down, the nakamal filled with the spirits of the dead. To make requests of them – big yams, healthy children, victory over rivals – Tanna men spat a little of their kava onto the ground. Not an offering, he stressed, because the dead had their own kava, the tamafa was more like a knock on the door. I'd done it perfectly last night.

I was delighted, but felt obliged to be truthful. 'It was just a mistake.'

The Chief suggested they make more kava, right away, so that they could see whether it was true.

'No, really – it was a mistake,' I said hastily. Losing my kava virginity last night had been an unsettling experience, one I hadn't yet had a chance to come to grips with. I hoped for a few days' respite before the next jaw-grinding, petrol-scented root-juice session. 'Anyway,' I reasoned, looking straight at Kal, 'if I'd been here before, I'd know about the volcano making the ground shake, wouldn't I?'

Kal and his father conducted a muttered conference. The Chief sniffed the air in a particularly magisterial way. 'But you brought us clay pipes. And as you drank, we watched you look across at...' – he licked his lips and glanced theatrically at the cloud-swaddled mountain behind us – 'at that hill as well.'

'Tukosmwera?'

As one, the village gave a gasp. Chief Jack's eyes narrowed. He spoke in a quiet, trembling voice. 'How do you know the name of that hill?'

'Just like the pipes, I read it in a book. I mean – not a book. Some letters from Prince Philip. I have them here in my bag.'

'Show them to me,' commanded the Chief. Despite the quavering voice and the way his hairdo rose like mist from a mountainside, he was very good at giving orders. I could see why he'd become a chief.

'Not exactly from Prince Philip,' I clarified, rummaging through my bag. 'From his office. His Secretary. The man who writes his letters.'

'In Buckingham Palace?'

'Yes.'

'Give them.'

I handed over the sheaf of many-times photocopied pages from the Duke of Edinburgh's Personal Secretary at the time, the splendidly named Brigadier Sir Miles Hunt-Davis. After repeated pestering from me, the Brig had sent some of the early correspondence between Port Vila-based civil servants and the Palace at the time the first photograph was donated. It included a brief summary of the cult, written by Kirk Huffman, and an outline of the major myths.

I watched as my little archive was divvied up and pored over by the village, huddling in packs over sheets of paper they couldn't read. Chief Jack thrust one of them back at me.

'Read it.'

It was a myth – the central myth of the movement, in fact. I started to read. 'A boat sailed past – three-masted, red, black and white,' I began cautiously.

The men waved at me, irritated. 'Stand up!' cried the Chief. I did as he said, with apologies. Speech-making on Tanna was a weighty business – never to be approached in a casual way. I continued with the myth:

'Inside sat the King. Sometimes he wore a captain's uniform, a suit of gold and silver, sometimes he was a cowboy. He was sailing to Aneityum, down past the south-western side of Tanna.

'As the boat sailed past the rock called Nuaru, a man from a nearby village was sitting by the sea. This man knew that the kava speaks to us only when we are quiet. So he sat alone, close to the rock, drinking the kava his son had prepared for him.

'The kava made the man see. And he watched as the King came to stand on the deck of his boat, gazing out at Tanna. He was strong and tall – a man who rode a white horse, a man who fought in World War Two – but his face was sad.'

I glanced at the Chief, his mahogany face cracked with concentration as he rocked back and forth on his horn-hard heels.

'The King's wife came to stand by him, on his left-hand side. The man on the beach heard her, because he was drinking kava.

'"My dear," asked the King's wife, "tell me what is wrong."

'"I have to tell you a secret," the King said. He pointed to the rock, Nuaru. 'The name of that rock is Nuaru. In my language, it means, "I am coming."'

'"What language?"

'"The language of that place," the King replied, "and of all the villages that lie behind the rock, of the mountain you can see above them. That is my home. Its name is Tukosmwera. My father is there. I am not a white man. I am from Tanna, and one day I will leave you and return. I am coming back to that rock, and when I put my foot on it, mature kava roots will spring from the ground, the old men will become young again, and there will be no more sickness or death."

'When she heard this, his wife knew that it was true, and she began to cry. And the man on the shore heard and saw it all.'

As I finished, the crowd slapped their shins in applause. The Chief waved a finger at them to be quiet.

'This came to you from Prince Philip?'

'No. Yes. It came from here. Somebody told this story to a man who worked here, and he told Prince Philip.'

'When?'

'At the time you were angry, because the government man had made you unhappy, and you asked for something from the British government to make you glad again.'

'ah yes. *Man belong gavman.* Mr Wilkie,' Chief Jack said, repeating one of the names he'd mentioned last night. 'One time Mr Wilkes … another time Mr Wilkie.'

I wondered what he was indicating. Some wordplay on the name of this government administrator? Some link to an earlier or later man with a similar name?

'We gave Mr Wilkie a pig,' the Chief went on. 'He didn't give anything back.'

He was referring to the Resident Commissioner, Mr Alexander Mair Wilkie. 'In 1966. I know,' I said. 'And about eleven years later the British government realised you were angry. So they wanted to know about you, and the things you believed, so a man called Kirk Huffman wrote a letter about it to Buckingham Palace. And then, a long time later, Prince Philip's Secretary told me.'

'Cook Gavman,' mused the Chief. 'Yes, that man is my friend. You call him Kirk Huffman. But we know his name is Cook Gavman,' he continued, stressing the last word, which meant 'government' in Bislama. 'Because he is a gate. For the end of the time of the white men, which lasted from Captain Cook, to the time now, the time of the government, see?'

'Erm ... OK.'

'We told Cook Gavman what we wanted, and through him, Prince Philip spoke to us.'

This was close to the historical record. During the seventies an Australian businessman named Bob Paul had developed an affectionate relationship with the men of the Yaohnanen area. In discussions with them he'd been told their local mountain was occupied by a spirit called Kalbaben. He had many famous sons, among them the Duke of Edinburgh. And some token of the latter, they said, would compensate for the insult they'd been dealt over the pig. On his next trip to Port Vila, Bob Paul told the British Residency, who were preparing to leave for good as the New Hebrides became independent. They, in turn, consulted anthropologist Kirk Huffman, whose report into the matter was sent straight to the Palace.

As a result, on 21 September 1978, the same day Pope John Paul I was found dead in his chambers after a reign of only forty-four days, a new religion joined the ranks. The photograph was presented by a delegation from the British Residency, along with five clay pipes. In the enigmatic complaints of the past decade, the elders of Yaohnanen had employed the broken pipe metaphor to express their feelings about the treatment of kastom. There was kava and dancing and a speech, in which the last Resident, Andrew Champion, told the Tannese that Britain would never forget them. The BBC had intended to film it all, but their correspondent had enjoyed so many shellfuls of island hospitality that he was incapable of the task. The French, meanwhile, sent a scathing report on the affair to Paris, accusing their counterparts of political chicanery.

That wasn't the end of it. Tuk Noao, a Yaohnanen seer, whose tribal title 'Voice of the Canoe' made him roughly equivalent to a Minister of Information, set a test to make sure that the signed photograph of Prince Philip had come from him, carving a ceremonial pig-killing club and sending it to the Duke with a further request. After careful consultation with Kirk, Prince Philip sent back another photograph, in which he wore a sober charcoal suit, stood in the grounds of Buckingham Palace and brandished the club – called a nalnal – in impeccable kastom fashion. Their doubts allayed, the leading lights of Philippism offered the Duke three virgins as wives, if only he'd return to his village. Kwin Lisbet, his current wife, could come too, they added. Nervous officials now advised the Royal Family to stay away from Tanna, advice followed ever since.

But another photograph was sent, and more letters passed between Buckingham Palace and that distant mountain village. All of which, as Prince Philip and his advisers knew full well, acted to encourage a group of people in a belief that was untrue. I still wanted to know why. And why the belief had come about in the first place.

Meanwhile, though, I had a troubled Chief to appease. Keen-eyed, cocking his head to ensure he grasped every last detail, the old man had me repeat the main myth, slowly. Then he had me read all the others: tales of Prince Philip and his wayward brother, Jake Raites, of his journey across the seas to Europe, of all the miracles he had already wrought for the people of Tanna. And one thing became diamond clear. Neither the Chief, nor anyone in his village, had heard a word of them.

'Problem,' he said neatly.

But he said the word looking over my shoulder, and when I followed his cloudy gaze I saw an inebriated Nako loping into the village, his arm around Siyaka. The pair collapsed, owl-eyed, in the midst of our group, with the air of gate-crashers convinced that no one has seen them. They were misguided in this. Chief Jack delivered a thundering rebuke upon their heads, and they winced under its force, although, before it concluded, they also started to titter. Siyaka, today sporting a sort of Dolly Parton get-up of denim and tassels, wiped his mouth with his wrist and straightened up. Nako, at some length, marshalled his lips into a state where they were capable of addressing me. But before he could manage this, Siyaka had joined me in chummy intimacy upon the bench.

'I like you,' he declared violently.

'I like you, too,' I replied. I watched as Siyaka picked up the microphone he'd knocked off the seat and bashed it curiously against the wood. I took it from him.

'Matthew,' he declared, with pious concentration. 'I like you because you have come to make the village great again,' he rambled. 'Like the time when the white men came and before Nako was...'

Nako shushed him. 'He has been drinking too much shells of kava,' he croaked at me robotically.

'Really?'

I returned my attention to the Chief, who was stabbing the point of his machete into the ground in unhappy distraction. He had me go once again through the section of the myth where Prince Philip's boat sailed past Aneityum. This had really happened, and it dated the story to the second royal visit to the area, in 1974.

'I saw him then,' Chief Jack said, his eyes misting over. 'Some of us went across to Vila, and I was in a canoe that rowed out to the ship to greet him.'

'What did Philip look like?' I asked, pointing the microphone towards him.

'Sad – like the story. But we know why. You call his house Buckingham Palace. But we know what it really means.' The Chief paused for dramatic effect. 'Back-e-go-home-paradise!' He clapped his hands. 'Because he is sick with longing for Tanna.'

Back-e-go-home-paradise, Cook Gavman. Wordplay, it seemed, was a major contributor to the Tannese brand of mysticism. I felt a pressing need to write this point down, a need that became considerably more pressing when I realised I didn't have my notebook with me. It then became positively depressing as I remembered exactly where that notebook was. Inside a plastic carrier bag, inside another bag, under the protective eye of a Port Vila motel owner. My spirits plummeted. I'd come all this way without a sodding notebook.

'We know he lives in a big house,' the Chief continued, unaware of my torment, 'with soldiers around it,

and when he rides in a truck, you cannot see him because the windows are made of darkness. Because he is
a tabu man.'

I tuned in to this bit. The word 'tabu' had been causing me trouble ever since I'd arrived in Vanuatu. I'd
imagined it to be riven with all sorts of threatening,
mystical associations, which didn't quite square with its
appearance at the back of restaurants and museums.
Yes, 'tabu' could sometimes just mean 'No Entry', but
here its meaning was different. Philip was a man set
apart, sacred and dangerous.

'Perhaps,' I offered, 'perhaps someone in another
village told these stories to Kirk Huffman?'

'And there are nakamals where they'd tell Cook
Gavman to put these stories on a piece of paper?' the
Chief cried. 'Ha!'

I supposed this was a copyright problem. Yaohnanen
regarded itself as rightful owner of everything under
the Prince Philip franchise. So the arrival of this collection of unknown stories, seemingly from Philip's hand
itself, was a blow to the foundations. Picture the mood
in the Vatican if it was discovered that some eleventh
commandment or fifth Gospel was being peddled on
the marketplaces of Jerusalem, well known to Copts
and Nestorians but a total mystery to those who saw
themselves as the guardians of the truth.

'All right,' the Chief chuntered on sourly. 'Maybe
Kowiya would do something like that. Maybe in Yakel.'

I looked blank, pretending not to know who he meant. Now, I thought, was not the time to mention my own bit of business with Chief Kowiya.

'We must all drink kava together, to see if the kava will give an answer.'

I groaned inwardly. Could no single half-hour go by on this island without me being required to sink a bucket of electric golly? How did any anthropologist get any work done when they were required to please local etiquette by getting out of their skulls from sunrise to bedtime?

Then an idea struck me. 'Maybe I could find out for you?' Possibly, on Tanna, with its mind-warping mesh of ever-shifting loyalties, a visitor might find out more about this mysterious case of myth theft than someone from the aggrieved village itself.

'You should certainly visit the other villages,' Chief Jack decreed, after much thought. 'Then you might learn something. Nako will help you.'

I glanced at Nako, who'd chosen that very moment to glance at me. It was a difficult look to read, combining bashfulness with something else, redolent of cats and cream. He scooped up the photocopied myths almost greedily.

I felt pleased to have a mission, though. Today hadn't gone so well. I saw there was a basic link to Prince Philip, and a way of interpreting real facts about him – the name of his house, his visits to the area – so as to bolster an underlying idea of him as a Tannese exile. But I'd seen nothing that could be called a religion, nor heard any mention of the longed-for cargo. Chief Jack's press archive wasn't a sacred object – he seemed happy for me to leaf through it, and left it fluttering on the ground for some time afterwards.

Then there were the signed photographs sent by the Palace – two in 1978, a more recent one in 2000, depicted by various visiting journalists as veritable icons, proudly displayed on the boundaries of the village as a badge of the still-burning faith. But not now, apparently. The only thing on the edge of the village now was a great dolorous pig, being fattened up in a pen.

'Could I start with a look at the photographs?'

'They are in another place,' the Chief said quickly, bending one of his needle-thin legs underneath the other.

'Can I see them?'

The Chief looked down. He murmured something to Nako. 'You said you would find about the stories,' Nako chipped in, his voice thick. The Chief pointed at my microphone and said something else. 'When you go to ask the people in the other places,' Nako continued, staring at the ground, 'you put their voices into that camera and you give it to my father.' He gazed at me intently.

A deal was being offered here: my donkeywork and technology in return for the innermost secrets of the

Philip cult. The voice recorder, I imagined, was desired so that the Chief could store and replay the evidence of his neighbours' betrayal, should it be found. It was just as everyone had told me it would be – no knowledge for free. I nodded and the Chief smiled serenely.

'We will show both of them to you soon.'

'I thought there were three photographs.'

'Three?'

'Yes, two of Prince Philip sitting, and one of him holding the nalnal.'

'The nalnal?' repeated the Chief warily.

'Yes, the club for killing pigs, the nalnal that Tuk Noao made and sent back to…'

'Wait a minute… How do you know about *him?*'

At this point Siyaka, who had been absent-mindedly chipping at a charred log with his machete, succeed in dislodging a small section of it, only to realise, as it flew through the air, that it was red-hot. He gave a shout, but this failed to prevent the ember from landing on the rear end of a sleeping dog, which then went mad and bit a nearby child, turning the whole scene into a veritable opera of crying, barking, chasing, waving and spitting. In the midst of this the Chief declared with regal outrage that he'd had quite enough and was going back to bed. This he did, accompanied by the piglet, and the crowds departed so that, some five minutes after, there remained only myself and the still form of Nako, blinking at a log.

We grinned at one another and I felt, at this moment, a little glad that I'd be working with him, so offered him some gum. He took it and stuck it in his hair, before informing me that I'd made a dreadful, unforgivable mistake.

'What did I do?'

'You cannot talk about Tuk Noao,' he slurred emphatically. Today he was wearing one of his loudest floral shirts, with high-waisted black slacks and a pair of sunglasses lodged in the woolly mesh of his hair. The thing he most resembled was a dance teacher, and the effect of this look, deep in the bush lands of the South Pacific, was unsettling. 'No Tuk Noao here,' he repeated.

'I thought he was a friend of your father.'

'Yes. You can talk of Tuk,' Nako decreed, patting his piece of gum. I rather wished I hadn't given it to him. 'But you cannot speak that his hands made the nalnal that was given to the Prince Philip.'

'Why not?'

Nako gazed at me coolly. 'Because my father is the one. Not Tuk Noao.'

I scratched my head. 'But Tuk *did* make the nalnal, didn't he?'

Nako winced. 'You cannot *speak* that,' he repeated, rising and walking away.

It was a fitting end to an interview characterised throughout by utter confusion. I had no means of writing anything down. I'd taken on a new mission in the midst of being unable to start my first. I'd offered my services to the Chief without knowing what the consequences might be if I failed to deliver. I'd partnered up with Nako, which, I suspected, without exactly knowing why, might make things twice as hard. I'd scandalised local sensitivities by implying that a certain man carved a pig-killing club, a statement which seemed to be true, yet also wrong. And what the hell did Ken Dodd have to do with it all?

Nako turned back and said there was a dance in the next village. Some of the men there were quite old, and they might remember the beginnings of the Prince Philip cult. It would be an excellent place to start our enquiries.

'Is it a long walk?' I said, shouldering my bag.

Nako snorted. 'We're not going today.' He sucked his teeth at the sheer silliness of the idea. 'Today we have to do something else.'

'What?'

'Today,' he declared happily, 'today we have to drink kava.'

He took me to a neat, proud little village called Ioknaauka, just down the hill. It was where the Norwegian anthropologist Vigestad had stayed twenty-five years ago, and they all still spoke of him with warmth. Ioknaauka looked like the sort of place that might win a Village of the Year award, with its trimmed bushes, its tidy dancing ground and its spiffy little wooden rack for the men to store their kava shells. Yaohnanen looked forlorn and gimcrack by comparison and I had a sense, not for the first time, that the Chief's village, in spite of its importance in the cult, might have lost out or fallen behind in some vital way. I wondered if I could ever find out why.

On the way back up the hill, Nako showed me a sandalwood tree: a tall, spindly thing with tiny leaves. He said: 'This was why you came.'

'Did I?' Was it a cultic tree? I wondered. Might it have some vital role in Philip worship?

I could get no more sense out of him but later, left alone in the dead of the afternoon with my books, I got an inkling of what Nako had meant. The tree wasn't why I'd come, but why my ancestors had: a magnet for a new wave of white incomers, looking for sandalwood to sell to the Chinese for their incense sticks.

The trade, so the history books told me, needed no particular skills beyond brute force and greed. It could be practised in rickety old vessels fit for the scrapyard, with the crews sharing generous profits. The promise of juicy dividends drew adventurer-capitalists to Tanna by the shipload, and between 1825 and the 1860s the history of contact bristles with unpleasant incidents. The most infamous concerned an expedition of American and Australian ships, staffed with a Tongan crew. They'd started badly, shooting a man while gathering sandalwood on Erromango, just north of Tanna. They then sailed farther north to Efate, where they quarrelled with locals about their rights to take the wood. Shots were fired, the locals fled to some caves. The Tongans pursued them and made fires at the entrance to the caves, suffocating sixty-eight people in a slow, ghastly fashion.

The price of the perfumed cargo fluctuated wildly over the nineteenth century: up to £50 a ton at times, down to two at others. The locals couldn't understand this; it became another feature of the weirdness of Whitefella – generous one summer, hard-bitten the next, so impossible to classify. The traders exploited local rivalries by kidnapping men from Tanna and selling them to their arch-enemies, the Erromangans, in exchange for the precious wood. The Tannese were duly dined upon. Another trick was to kidnap a chief and hold him to ransom until his people handed over all their wood. Except they didn't always hand him over – they might offer him to an enemy group in exchange for more of the scented cargo.

The traders also dabbled in biological warfare. In 1861 the schooner *Bluebell* took Tannese men with measles and landed them on Erromango, with one-third of the island's population dying as a result. Their motives were often to spoil the possibilities of trade for other sandalwooders in the area. One captain's account describes a ship's mate taking potshots at the shoreline as they sailed away with their wood, killing six men and ensuring that the next Europeans to arrive would get a chilly reception. Or one that was far too warm.

But skulduggery was mutual. When the British ship *Sovereign* was wrecked off the shore of Efate, her twenty-man crew was rescued by friendly locals, who then ate all but two of them. It was also common practice to mix hollow logs in with the sandalwood. Some villages performed an elaborate sting operation – loading up all the sandalwood on the beach to entice traders in, taking the payment, and then snaffling it all back before it could be taken to the waiting ships.

And not every European was a pirate. From 1843, men like Captain James Paddon and Robert Towns established the first permanent white settlements in the Vanuatu area, trading sandalwood, supplying visiting ships and rearing cattle. This kind of permanent presence would have been impossible if they'd behaved unscrupulously. The locals would have had them for lunch.

By the end of the 1840s there was a sandalwood mountain sitting fragrantly in various oriental dockyards and prices fell. Many prospectors headed to California, to participate in the Gold Rush. It was also becoming harder to get hold of the stuff itself. The Europeans had acted like a tribe of nomads, parking up in some nice, verdant valley, stripping it of all they needed and then buggering off. Aneityum, to the south of

Tanna, had been picked clean. The forests of Efate and Tanna itself were greatly depleted, their finely tuned ecosystems never to recover.

The Englishman Leonard Cory, who set up home on Tanna in 1849, left behind the first records of guns being traded in exchange for sandalwood. He also took pigs as payment, which he then traded with the Erromangans. While there was nothing outstandingly unscrupulous about Mr Cory, he sums up what the sandalwood period achieved: introducing a deadly new weapon and meddling with the traditional economy.

Once again, the locals were left scratching their heads about this latest encounter with Whitefella. He came, obsessed with a tree that was useless to him, he grabbed and he went away. Would he come back? The answer was yes – this time driven by new goals. From the 1840s, contact would no longer be sporadic, but concerted, and the rhythm of life in the islands would never return to its predictable beat.

CHAPTER THREE

An Encounter with Nakwa, Serpent God, Satan, Causer of Wet Dreams. Or Someone a Bit Like Him

I JUMPED awake, sweating and cold. My shirt was on back to front and I smelt like an expired leg of ham. A tiny fire was hissing inside the hut. Nako lit these because, like all his brethren, he needed the searing hot kiss of wood smoke in his lungs and eyes on a round-the-clock basis. His face had the creepy look of an amateur waxwork in the flickering flame. Kal was squatting with him in the dark, both men drawing on clay pipes.

'Sorry,' Nako croaked. 'They are burn the baby.'

'What?'

'The woman belong Kal. They are burn the baby now.'

I swallowed sharply, tasting the wood and their dank tobacco. Burn the baby? I must have that wrong, surely.

Nako spat on the floor. Kal spat into the fire. Nako spat into the fire, too, and the flames went out. He swore. And then spat.

Spitting was not solely a spiritual activity on Tanna, but also a sport and performance art. All day long, cigarettes made from newspaper were smoked in the nakamals and these, plus the musty kava, the constant billowings of volcanic ash and the fibrous leavings of the sugar canes he chewed left the average son of Tanna with some disagreeable tastes in the mouth. Hence the spitting. Practice made perfect, and the ti-niest nipper was able to eject the juices of his mouth in a neat jet, which then landed somewhere with a satisfying splat or twang. I'd been trying myself, and so far succeeded only in covering the Chief, a pretty young girl and my own leg with generous servings of spittle.

'Sorry for waking up you *pphwt*,' Nako said, round-ing off his apology with a basic, no-frills, intra-conver-sational kind of gob. 'Tssss,' it went, as it sizzled on the glowing log.

'*Pphwt!*' added Kal. At night, owing to the kava, the men adjusted their personal spit settings from 'fre-quent' to 'constant'.

'Sorry also *pphwt* that we smoke these pipes *pphwt*,' added Nako.

'Your father said they were to be given to the Big Men.'

'Yes. *Pphwt*,' Nako confirmed. He didn't seem to have anything to add on the subject, and I couldn't see the merits of debating it, so I wished the two men sweet dreams and turned over. I wondered, with a shiver, what constituted a sweet dream for Kal, who had beadily watched me for the duration of that little exchange, stroking the clipped ends of his moustache. Was it me, *qua me*, he disliked, I mused, or just the fact of me being a foreigner on his turf?

I fell asleep finally, and by the time I stirred again, Nako was nowhere to be found. This didn't surprise me – he was never in the hut in the mornings, usually returning, from some unstarted business, around the midday mark. I sometimes, rather unkindly, imagined there might be a café just over the hill, where my little companion was filling up on eggs and bacon. It was a vision influenced by my own diet, consisting solely of dry-baked yams the size of a man's arm and presented twice a day with a proud flourish by the Chief himself. Back in Sydney I'd asked Kirk Huffman to tell me the most essential item an anthropologist could take to Tanna and he'd baffled me by saying it was Worcestershire Sauce. Now I understood why.

After tripping over my shoulder bag, which lay openmouthed in the doorway of the hut, I emerged into a glorious morning, the sunshine causing the moisture to boil away in sheets of potting-shed vapour. The Mystical Bush Orchestra was in full flow again, a chorus of faerie toots and peeps winging in from all regions of the forest. I resolved that, today, if I did nothing else, I'd find out who was behind them.

I mounted the steep, muddy slope to the water tap, arranging my clothes on a nearby thorn bush. The stubborn downpour of recent days had rendered further investigations impossible, and I'd spent the time in the nakamal with the men, who had adopted me as a sort of odd but principally harmless mascot. Sheltering under leaves from the rain, we'd discussed five topics in great depth: yams, pigs and kava, whether you could get them in Britain, and if not, why not. They'd also told me of the gods who populated the nara wol, the other world beyond the one we see. Of Wunghen, the creator god, who'd fashioned the pig because he was lonely, then abandoned it because of its sloppy eating habits. Of the slippery serpent god Nakwa, who sometimes appeared in the guise of a Frenchman, and whose curses were politics and money and wet dreams. And the fierce Kalbaben, who tore wayward children apart with his claws and his razor-teeth.

All the men – from the shy teenagers to the old Chief – insisted that Kalbaben's son was Prince Philip, and that he'd come from the golden-sloped mountain we saluted with every kava shell. But this was the upper limit of what they would offer. With an acrobatic deftness, they were able to flip each question session so that they were questioning me. At this stage the sum total of my learning on the Prince Philip cult could be written in triplicate on a fingernail.

So I was delighted this day had begun with sunshine. Our presence was requested in the neighbouring village of Iatanas, where a dance was to be held when the rains finished, and some old men might know something of the matters which puzzled me. I was less pleased, on stripping naked and turning on the water tap, to discover that nothing came out. I twisted it this way and that, but to no avail.

I dressed crabbily in my stiff clothes and padded back down the slope. Nako was waiting, a smoking yam in one hand, my bag in the other, and upon his sturdy breast a T-shirt bearing the faded image of late-eighties rock combo T'Pau.

'We have to go to see the dance,' he said. He handed me the yam and my bag. I made to sit down, but Nako said, 'We go now.'

So we walked together through a grove of dripping mandarin trees, accompanied part of the way by a charming piglet. En route, through stultifying mouthfuls of yam, I asked Nako if this was a Prince Philip dance we were about to attend, or one associated with some other faith. 'We have to see the dance,' he replied baldly. 'I will guide you there, and introduce you to the people and we will look at the dance.'

I suspected Nako had been downing those daybreak kava shells again. But most of my dealings with him were turning out like this. He took the role of guide seriously, bustling me about, informing me what was going on and re-informing me some minutes later, even if nothing had changed. But while I'd developed a jokey relationship with many of the men, the one I spent most time with still held himself apart. In Port Vila, as we tramped the town for supplies, I'd seen him stopping on every street corner to slap hands or make a uniquely Melanesian kissing sound with lips and teeth at people he knew, but I'd felt little of that bonhomie radiating towards me. It was just my uneasy status, I decided, that was the cause: somewhere between charge and boss, burden and patron. He'd shown interest in my watch and my aftershave, and I'd said he could have both of them when I left the island. This, and the sheer act of our spending every day and night together, I trusted, should help things to improve. Either that, or he just thought I was a twat.

'Do you carry with you those stories from the Prince Philip?' Nako asked suddenly, as we crossed a wooden cattle grid over a chuckling brook.

'In the bag,' I said, adding automatically, 'and they're not from Prince Philip – they were sent by his secretary... Nako, what's that noise in the trees?'

'The music? It is just the boys,' Nako said, vaguely. 'Hiss Sekreturry,' he pondered further. 'What is the name of that man?'

'Brigadier Sir Miles Hunt-Davies,' I said. 'But what do you mean – the boys?'

'Briga what?'

I repeated it. Nako rolled the words around his mouth.

'Big Ass Dear Summer Lance Daisies,' he pronounced finally. 'Ha ha ha.' His stout chest heaved with laughter. 'Ha ha ha ha ha ha ha.' He slapped me on the back, his body convulsed by high-pitched, almost girlish giggles. 'Funny name. Ha ha ha. Ha ha ha.'

Dropping the remains of the yam, and my questions about the Mystical Youth Orchestra along with it, I joined in his laughter. And the two of us were chuckling away when a pair of severe-looking men stepped into our path and stayed there. Furnished with pistols and capes, they might have been a pair of highwaymen. Nako shook their hands, they treated me to a short, essentially unfriendly glance, and some words were traded. Without warning, the taller of the two men – whose T-shirt advertised an establishment in Canberra called Bazza's Sango-Shack – suddenly placed his two palms against Nako's chest and pushed him into a bush. There were no cries, no shouts, and no further gestures. The two men flitted past me down the damp path, and Nako floundered in a bed of prickly things.

'What was that about?' I asked, helping him up.

'I just know them,' Nako said breezily, as he removed a jagged thorn from his arm.

'Are they from our village?'

'Just make funny with me, it's all,' Nako said quietly. 'Come on.'

I trotted after him. 'But they've cut your arm.'

Nako glanced at his arm, beaded with blood that shone green under the canopied sky. 'Just friends,' he repeated coldly.

Baffled, I followed him through an archway of complex bush-work into a wide, breezy meeting place. A number of Yaohnanen men were already squatting and spitting there, including the Chief and Kal.

'You are very late,' the Chief observed, even though no activities – apart from squatting and spitting – appeared to be taking place. Then he added, on seeing my face, 'What's the matter?'

'We just met these two men… ' I began breathlessly.

'He is very tired,' Nako interrupted, giving me a forbidding stare. 'Aren't you very tired?' I fell quiet and stared at my blackened feet. It felt like a rebuke. It also felt like Nako was hiding something. His hand, I noticed, remained over the cut on his forearm.

'We must wait here now,' Nako pronounced, making himself comfortable amid a pile of rocks. 'The people inside of the village they are not ready.' I couldn't see how he knew this, as he'd not had any contact with the people in the village, but I decided to leave it alone. The Chief bade me join him and as I did so, gave a theatrical shiver, to underline the point that it was cold.

It was always cold on Tanna, and the men were always complaining about it. Anthropologists, I thought, often made a mistake in assuming that every human culture was inherently sensible and logical. A rain dance, for example, doesn't really make rain – not in the view of social scientists anyway – but forces conflicting factions within a tribe to cooperate. A neat idea, except that, within the same tribe, you'll find a dozen examples of blinding stupidity. Back in the days of inter-tribal warfare on Tanna, it was customary for one village to give the limbs of its slaughtered enemies to its neighbours. But, because of the rules of exchange on Tanna, those neighbours had to return the gesture, obtaining the body parts to do so by waging war on someone else. There wasn't a great deal of sense in that. Nor in the constant shivering and moaning of Man Tanna, who'd had a few thousand years to get used to the weather, and develop weaving, but simply hadn't.

'English weather!' the Chief said.

'I brought it with me,' I joked.

'You know how to do that?'

Tanna was not the place where you could make quips like this. 'No, I just meant…'

'Tanna has the same weather as your country because the two islands were joined together,' the Chief countered. 'Everyone knows this.' The half-dozen men around us signalled their agreement.

'Some people say Tanna was joined to Africa. That's why there are black men there. That's why we call Africa "Hafrica", you see, because it is only half of a place. But here, in Yaohnanen, we know Tanna was joined to your country. That's why the weather's so bad. That's why we try to bring them together.'

I sensed some central membrane of Tannese thought taking shape here. I remembered what Siyaka had said on that first night, about every Man Tanna having a doppelganger somewhere else. 'Bring them together. You mean – you can make them join up again?'

The Chief assumed a patient tone with me. 'You can't make two islands join back together again.' He spoke over his shoulder to the rest of the party. 'Not even Kowiya can do that, with all his money!'

A rumble of laughter greeted this point, and I cleared my throat. 'About Chief Kowiya…'

'No, it cannot be done,' the Chief interrupted. 'We just walk slowly and we build roads.'

'Walk slowly and build roads?'

'You'll see. The Hebrides – tell me – you have some islands called the Hebrides, don't you?' In his accent, it sounded like *Hey-pretties*.

'Yes, they're off the coast of Scotland.'

'And the main town of Scotland is?'

'Edinburgh.'

'And the old name for this place, here?' the Chief shot back. 'The name your people gave it?'

'Erm… New Hebrides.'

The Chief sat back, folding his arms with a smile. 'And another name for Prince Philip is?'

'The Duke of … Oh.'

My open-mouthed expression caused a ripple of laughter around the nakamal. The Chief nodded graciously, like some withered Zen Master of the mountain tops, whose disciple had finally shown signs of progress. 'You'd better write it down,' he added. 'White men are bad at remembering things.'

All was not entirely lost on the note-making front. Having rummaged through the hut the night before, I'd alighted upon a packet of cheap postcards, purchased in Sydney. I'd intended to record various little pen-portraits of Tannese life upon them and then post them to Prince Philip when I returned to Port Vila. But they were now drafted in to compensate for the absence of a notebook. I had twelve of them, and I was writing in eye-wateringly small script, a tough task when you are excited.

It was the first indication I'd had that Philippism still thrived in this place, and that it had some philosophical backing. As with the early Gnostics and the Kabbalists, there was a notion of an imperfect world, ruptured and disintegrated. There had once been unity and harmony – within men and continents. Then some cosmic rift had occurred, a splitting apart of lands and people. Tanna became separated from some parent land mass, Tanna men exiled from their doppelgangers. This was how, perhaps, a black princeling from the New Hebrides had ended up trapped in the old ones, a son of Kalbaben become this white Prince Philip. The islands could never be physically reunited, but Chief Naiva and his cohorts seemed to imagine something could be done. Walking slowly, he'd said. Building roads. You'll see, he'd said. But I still didn't.

And why had he chosen this morning to lay this before me? Because he was slowly beginning to trust me, or because of the ritual we were about to witness? I turned to ask him, but he was now locked in a low-voiced conversation with his son. Everyone else was dozing in the grass, or staring up at the trees. Nobody seemed in the least bit concerned to get on with their day.

Yet, for all their leisure, they were hard workers, the Tannese, and I'd heard they'd been highly sought after for their strength and endurance by the plantation owners in an earlier, sadder chapter of the island's history. With little else to do as we waited for the ritual, I hauled out a book and read about it.

It all started with the American Civil War, disrupting cotton supplies and creating a spike in prices. In 1863 Captain Robert Towns, a wealthy Sydney merchant, decided to cash in by setting up a cotton plantation at Brisbane. He staffed it with islanders from the New Hebrides, thereby inventing a new business.

Blackbirding, as it came to be known, was not always slavery. But it was rarely much better. Towns's first load of workers came to him courtesy of one Ross Lewin, a man of piratical reputation, later murdered for land-grabbing on Tanna.

The cotton gig didn't last long when peace returned to the United States. But Australian planters began to invest in sugar cane, which also needed a constant supply of fresh labour. Recruiters swarmed into the New Hebrides, using a variety of methods to entice people aboard their ships. Some went for theatre: one man had a costume with a large, waterproof bag underneath it. He would appear to drink huge quantities of salt water, until his belly bulged out like a pregnant hog's. Another used to amaze the crowds with his wooden leg, into which he shot bullets and stabbed swords. He was eventually forced to terminate this act when a native scientist tested the recruiter's apparent indestructibility by stabbing a knife into his bum.

Kidnapping was another recruiting strategy. In one case a blackbirder impersonated an Anglican clergyman and invited people on board to meet 'the Bishop'. They met, instead, with a blow on the head, before being locked in the hold and spirited off for long spells of indentured labour. Ships would sometimes surround and cut off local fishing expeditions, hauling their prey on board with boathooks. Another trick was to entice people onto the ship, then threaten to land them on

some rival island where they would certainly be killed –
forcing them to sign up for the plantations instead.

But plenty of New Hebrideans went willingly. Some
saw it as a handy escape route from a local vendetta,
the unbending tyranny of the village elders, the suf-
focation of a loveless marriage. It was a chance to see
the world and earn some money. Returnees came back
with a suit of clothes, a musket, knives and axes.

They didn't always come home to a warm welcome,
though. Sometimes the ships dumped them back on
any old island, where the locals might kill and eat them
on sight. Long memories meant that old scores had not
been forgotten: one woman from Tongoa came home
jubilantly, only to be hanged for having fled years ago
without permission. Another returnee from Erromango hanged himself, after reaching his village and finding his entire family dead from European-introduced
infections.

The recruiters weren't permitted to sail around entirely unchecked. In 1868 the Polynesian Labourers
Act set a minimum wage and tried to lay down guide-
lines about their basic rights. With the force of the law
behind him, Captain George Palmer seized a recruiting
ship off the coast of Fiji. It had paperwork claiming that
fifty-eight labourers were on board, headed for Sydney.
Palmer found 108, heading somewhere quite different.
The captain and crew of the ship were taken to Australia to face kidnapping charges. But the Melanesians on

board were not allowed to give evidence in court, and the magistrate ruled in the ship's favour. As an additional snub, Palmer was ordered to pay costs.

From 1871, every recruiting ship was supposed to carry a Government Agent, a churchwarden figure keeping a check on the practices of the crew. But the agents were often recruited by the very men who had a vested interest in maintaining a steady flow of cheap labour to the plantations. If anyone did report dodgy dealings, he was likely to lose his job.

Blackbirding slowed to a trickle in the 1880s, strangled by tighter legislation and a slump in sugar prices. From 1890, no more licences were issued to recruiters. In 1901 the 'White Australia' policy prevented more foreign labour coming in. In the meantime islands had been emptied, communities torn apart and mistrust between the races congealed into contempt. I pictured Man Tanna, watching the last of the blackbirders leaving, making the tamafa by spitting on his soil and praying no more white men would come. His prayer would remain unanswered.

I read on for a while, learning about the next, unwelcome wave of Europeans to land on Tanna, until a noise disturbed me. 'Stop looking at your bible,' the Chief said. I looked up, to see the entire village of Iatanas surging through the trees to greet us, singing hymns, playing banjos and distributing flowers.

'Now see,' said the Chief, patting my arm.

Our hosts wrapped us in a beaming embrace of harmony, and led us by the hands up a short hill to their village, which lay on a slope in the sunlight. There they once again encircled us and performed a chant, slapping their bare feet on the earth so hard that the bushes shook in time. It was a nasal, echoing business, taken up by the women and men in turn. I could almost feel the spindrift on my cheeks as the music took me back to their ancestors, moving through the waves in their mighty hewn canoes. Having thirsted so long for some signs of worship, I could feel my body racked by internal, joyful sobs.

An elderly woman came whirling around us, brushing herself against our shoulders and shins. A small party of others, like her in brightly dyed grass skirts, made dramatic hand actions in our direction, either casting out devils or casting something in. I was in Anthropologist Heaven. A short, large-headed man in a Chelsea football shirt approached. He was the owner of two staring eyes and one, lonely dreadlock coiling from the crown of his head. 'We all love you,' he said to me. 'Please come with me.'

He led the Chief, Nako and me past the blackened and still-smoking shell of some large building, and thence to a throne inside a reed booth. Seated inside this regal cupboard, we were given garlands of flowers, and then wave upon wave of smiling children loaded our laps with coconuts and cooked yams, mandarins and peanuts. As the pile of bounty reached throat height, I realised this might be a traditional Tannese torture: death by produce.

'It is your seat,' said the large-headed man, adding that his name was Jimmy Yasu. 'A few months ago a friend of ours had a dream. It said we should burn down the church and build this instead, and then a white man would come and sit in it.'

Beyond the front of our little kiosk, the villagers had organised themselves into an outdoor prayer meeting upon a grassy knoll. A tall, prophetic-looking gentleman – his pink bomber jacket and wide moustache reminded me of Freddie Mercury – was haranguing the crowd and jabbing his finger at the evil in their midst. Periodically they called out, 'Sorry, brother!' and a man shook a tambourine.

Meanwhile the grass-skirted whirlers corkscrewed about in the background, emerging from their trances with suspicious regularity to make sure they weren't about to tread on a cockerel or crash into a child. Perhaps they had some executive role in reuniting what had been split apart – like whirling dervishes whose skirts scattered blessings. The Chief nodded approvingly as I made tiny, feverish notes on the reverse of a view of Sydney Opera House.

'Dancing is very good,' he observed.

'Will the dancing make Prince Philip come back?'

The Chief blinked in alarm. 'This?' He traded looks

with Yasu. 'This is nothing to do with Philip. This is to do with them.'

I gazed in confusion at the scene before me: the seated revival meeting, the Ladies' Whirling Circle, and now it seemed, elsewhere in the arena, an outbreak of free-form devotional jitterbug. Among this new splinter group I spotted Siyaka, dressed as if for Cowes Week in navy blazer and khaki shorts, jerking about, with each hand attached to a small boy. Seeing me, he waved, sending the attached child flying across the floor, and receiving a battery of curses from its mother.

'So who are they?'

'We are Unity,' replied Yasu.

'Ah.'

'*UNITY!*' he bellowed, just in case I hadn't caught it, the single dreadlock flapping like the fuse on a bomb.

The entire village responded with a roar, '*UNITY!*'

'We follow Prophet Fred,' Jimmy added.

'That explains that, then,' I said, putting my pen away.

I'd heard about Prophet Fred, or Fred Nase, as he was properly known. He broke with the official John Frum movement in 1999, when he began to predict the end of the world. Some four thousand of his followers joined him in the settlement of Ienekahi, on the slopes of Mount Yasur. It was disputed territory – having become depopulated, even though plenty of people in the area were still making use of the land. Fred, meanwhile, had a claim on the place because his father had been one of its last original inhabitants.

Complaints began to trickle in from Tanna's Sulphur Bay, the official HQ of the John Frum movement. The John Frum were a powerful force, represented in the Vanuatu Parliament, their offices, flying the Stars and Stripes, guarded by beefy lads in uniform. Their leader, Isaac Wan (Isaac I), had been on an official trip to the White House – for reasons never fully disclosed. And he wasn't happy with Fred. Fred told his followers that there would be no need for work at the end of the world. Accordingly, many of them consumed their crops and killed their pigs. The waiting thousands, perched on the slopes of the volcano, began to pillage local gardens to survive. One farmer reported the loss of fifteen cows to the breakaway cultists.

Fred's supporters didn't even desert him when the mystical date of 1 January 2000 came and went without any major ructions in the space-time continuum. They continued to base themselves up at Ienekahi until April 2003, their faith confirmed by various other of Fred's prophecies having come true. He said Mount Yasur would become violent and kill people. He said Lake Siwi would rise up and flood Sulphur Bay. He said women and children would have dreams and visions. All of which – either astonishingly or predictably, depending on your perspective – came true.

The law courts exhibited a robust indifference to Fred's prophetic powers, and in 2003 police arrested him and thirty-eight others, dispersing the settlement. But the movement was merely regrouping. Fred and his cohorts were released on bail, pending a trial date. In August of that year Fred's spokesman announced that the 'Unity' movement had replaced and abolished John Frum. Isac Wan issued a further statement disputing this.

And so the debate raged on, with two John Frum cults, and the new one dancing in its gaudy grass skirts ever closer to the edges of revivalist Christianity. Fred had a large entourage – including a woman he was said to have raised from the dead. It was also rumoured he had inherited the title of 'stamba belong yam' – the Mystical Minister of All Yams – from his father. With this title came the right to fix the ritual calendar, and there were rumours that Fred intended to make it fit in with the Christian one. The island's conservative elements – including Chief Jack – were alarmed by the idea, and the threat this posed to their traditions, but there was little they could do.

It struck me that kastom was always under threat, not just from outside, but from within. In a society where virtually every man has some potentially important ritual title, the possibility of power struggles is immense – especially when they line up behind religions. That row of churches I'd seen when we arrived here reminded me what a hotbed of jostling faiths this island was, and how hard that must be for groups who just want to stick to a simple, traditional way of life. If it was possible at all, I reasoned, it must have needed some radical strategy.

'You are the man from London? Do you know Scarborough? That is a place in London. I know about it. These people do not, though. They are very dirty and stupid people.'

My interlocutor was a furtive, full-bearded individual with small, yellow teeth and a houndstooth bomber jacket. He had slipped, without invitation, onto the seat next to me, exuding a powerful scent of diesel.

'I am a missionary,' he announced, flecking the outer edges of my ear with spittle. 'I come from Futuna. Have you been there?' Before I could answer, he went on, 'Do you need the toilet? They don't have one here. These people are very dirty. I am teaching them how to be clean, but it is difficult, because they are not intelligent. Do you know – when I first came here, they tried to kill me?'

'How surprising of them.'

'They dance like this every Wednesday,' he carried on, getting louder. 'Always in the daytime. He told them not to dance at night, because that's when women get stolen.'

'He? Do you mean Fred?' I asked.

'Hmm?' He seemed uninterested in my questions, more concerned with being heard.

Yasu nodded. He said that everyone there was living on the Holy Spirit. 'Fred told us to stop using magic stones,' he said, referring to the main instruments of gardening sorcery on Tanna. 'Because the stones can kill people. We just dance and pray like this and the Big Man makes the yams grow.'

It confirmed what I'd heard about Fred's mission: providing Tanna with a kastom-oriented Christianity, keeping the dancing, replacing the magic with prayer, the cargo dreams with Bible-based images of a land of plenty. It was even said Fred had converted to Pentecostalism when he was working on a fishing boat, and would one day reveal his true colours.

'Are you a missionary?' the Missionary interrupted. 'Have you heard of the London Missionary Society? They are a big organisation. I attended a conference of theirs in Fiji. In fact, I delivered a talk to them on the subject of...'

Yasu darted a glance at me. 'We heal people – all over the island,' he said quietly, but intensely. 'And we do the work of the spirit.'

'Yes, yes,' the Missionary interjected. 'They burnt down their church, you know, because Fred told them to. Says the Big Man doesn't need churches.'

'A few days ago a little boy was circumcised by the spirit,' Yasu countered, leaning in close. It felt like some scene from the marketplaces of third-century Rome – Christian and pagan shouting their wares in each of the believers' ears. 'Nobody touched him. Just spirit.'

To me, a spirit that went round circumcising people sounded rather disagreeable. It must have shown on my face, but looked like scepticism. Yasu said I could come and look at the boy. I wasn't sure if I wanted to examine a small boy's recently cut penis, but supposed I better had.

'He doesn't want to see that,' the Missionary said. 'He is a Big Christian, this man, aren't you? Yes. But these people have their customs. They are not like ours.'

'I would quite like to see it, actually.' But Yasu now seemed to be exchanging some words with Nako, and didn't hear.

'You see?' the Missionary cried, pointing rudely at two of the whirling women. 'Look at them dance in the grass skirts!'

I tried to go for a walk around the place, and to catch up with Siyaka. But the diesel-scented man of God attached himself to me, unnecessarily flapping small boys out of my way, and pointing out things I needed no help interpreting, like huts and grass skirts and guitars. Whenever he sensed me losing interest, he told me I was a Bigfella Witness and I had Power-Belong-Jesus-Christ, and when he wasn't doing that, he was alerting me, at top volume, to the stupidity of the villagers and the crudeness of their way of life. I wondered if the instructions to burn the church had really come from Prophet Fred, or if the villagers of Iatanas had just done it out of sheer despair, with the Missionary inside it. Maybe that was why he smelt of diesel.

His kind hadn't proved popular in November 1839, when the ship *Camden* landed at Tanna, carrying missionary John Williams, his assistant Harris and three Samoan teachers. They put the teachers ashore and tarried just long enough for an unpleasant bit of cultural contact. A shipmate describes it neatly: 'Upon my arrival, I saw a very large native making signs for Mr Harris to open his mouth, who acceded to the request, and the fellow immediately spat down his throat.'

A bad sign. But the Man Tanna wasn't hawking down Harris's throat to be offensive. As well as functioning as a prayer to the ancestors, spitting could ward off bad spirits. Harris was taken to be a ghost and the man, in his own idiom, was simply trying to bust him.

Gargling frantically, Williams and Harris sailed off for Erromango. Within minutes of their landing there, before they'd even so much as produced a pamphlet, the locals turned hostile and killed the two missionaries. Meanwhile the Samoans fared badly on Tanna. Assuming everyone with a black skin must be somehow related, the missionaries had neglected to investigate the differences between Melanesians and Polynesians. The Samoans were unused to the windy, rainy climate.

They were just as prone to malaria as Europeans. The locals regarded them as beneath contempt: black like them, but without pigs.

The Australian press reacted with horror to the killing of Williams and Harris. This was the first sign that a new age had dawned, one in which events in the far-flung Pacific could be telegraphed across the world. In time this improved communication gave white people an ever greater role in determining the fate of Man Tanna.

In July 1842 the London Missionary Society sent George Turner and Henry Nisbet to join the Samoans, who were all sick with fever. Nobody knew anything about Jesus. They were still walking around naked. Turner and Nisbet set to, building houses and acquiring some of the local languages. By October they'd begun a school for adults. It was regularly attended, except when there was a war on, which was often, and a much more thorough business since the introduction of the European musket two decades earlier.

Turner and Nisbet's difficulties were more theological than practical. The Tannese already had their own religion, an easy-going pantheon of spirits, always willing to budge up and make room for another. Their world view was also coloured by an infuriatingly healthy degree of Tanno-centrism. When Turner and Nisbet took them through the old, old story, from Adam and Eve right through to Revelation, the elders listened carefully. Then they said, 'Well done. But you got a few bits wrong.' To them, the Christian god was just another one of the many. And since Turner and Nisbet had access to this god, there was nothing mysterious about them at all – they were just skilled magicians.

Dysentery was their real undoing. Like missionaries everywhere, they knew that healing the sick made people more willing to listen to them. But they were powerless in the face of the epidemic sweeping the island. People began to mutter about them. If their god was so powerful and so good – why couldn't they get him to stop the sickness? (A matter that had, in more abstract form, troubled theologians since St Augustine was in short trousers.) Meanwhile, just doing what they could, mopping the brows and patting the hands of the dying, fuelled native suspicions. On Tanna, magicians cause illnesses as well as cure them. Suspected of being responsible for the outbreak of dysentery, and then of not removing it, Turner, Nisbet and the Samoans had to flee on board a passing whaling ship.

Meanwhile the Reverend John Geddie had established a church on Aneityum, to the south, and was doggedly converting his way through 3500 souls. A man of indomitable courage and dour Presbyterian outlook, Geddie was well known to the local trading ships, owing to his endearing habit of lecturing passing sailors about keeping the Sabbath. It became a popular pastime of theirs to deliver supplies and mail to him only on rainy Sundays. Geddie would sit steadfastly at prayer while his cargo got soaked on the beach.

In 1858 the Tannese met their match in their person of John G. Paton, a Scot, a showman and a dab hand at sensationalist journalism. His account of his time on Tanna is fascinating, not least for its lurid mantle of Victorian melodrama. Paton casts himself as a sturdy soldier of Christ, under assault from the heathen from day one. His first impressions of Tanna were as dour as only a Dumfries lad could make them. 'We found the Tannese to be painted Savages,' he wrote, 'enveloped in all the superstition and wickedness of Heathenism. All the men and children go in a state of nudity. They are exceedingly ignorant, vicious, and bigoted, and almost void of natural affection.' The chiefs let him settle, but only, he said, because they wanted his blankets and fish hooks. Paton's wife died within the year, and so fraught were his relations with the locals that he took to sitting up all night beside her grave, armed with a revolver, to prevent them from stealing the corpse. One night an attack was mounted, recounted in terms redolent of the penny shocker:

'Seven or eight savages raised their great clubs in the air. I heard a shout – Kill him! Kill him! One savage tried to seize hold of me, but leaping from his clutch I drew the revolver from my pocket, and levelled it as for use, my heart going up to my God. I said: "Dare to strike me, and my Jehovah God will punish you …

for hatred to his worship and people. We love you all."
They yelled in rage, and urged each other to strike, but
the Invisible One restrained them. At this moment occurred an incident which I trace directly to the interpo-
sition of God.'

The 'incident' was a tornado, obligingly sent by the
Invisible One. Paton legged it to Australia and made
£5000 re-telling his tale to rapt audiences. He returned
to Tanna on board HMS *Curacao*, a warship dispatched
for the express purpose of punishing the locals for at-
tacks on traders and missionaries. Paton's version of
ensuing events differs from that of others. He now cast
himself as a peacemaker. The Tannese chiefs allegedly
produced a letter begging him to intercede and promising that they would be good from now on. Paton
pleaded, with Shakespearean eloquence, on their
behalf to the captain. But all to no avail. He shelled the
island, then landed 170 men, who killed four Tannese
and smashed everything they could find.

Opinion was divided about this attack. The grim
Reverend Geddie, to his credit, was appalled by it. But
Paton's Church applauded his efforts. Some said he'd
urged the whole mission in the first place, so it was his
fault it went sour. The navy was more offended by this
idea than the accusation of butchering natives – as if a
mere missionary could tell the Royal Navy what to do!

But missionaries like Paton had their plus points.
They were vigorously opposed to the blackbirding

trade, and Geddie's overblown accounts alerted Australian and European audiences to the kidnapping and slavery. It was public opinion, expressed in the newspapers, driven by missionaries' accounts, which forced the British government to take a more active role in policing the region.

But the French, too, had been eyeing up the New Hebrides. They had annexed New Caledonia in 1853 and it made strategic sense to nab more territory, to prevent their new acquisition from being surrounded by non-French powers. Meanwhile more Europeans were establishing permanent bases in the New Hebrides. The Australian government noted with alarm how many seemed to be former French convicts. They worried that, should there be another Anglo-French war, the north-east coast of Australia might be attacked.

And events on Tanna made it clear that some permanent authority was needed. In 1874 the piratical recruiter Ross Lewin had been shot dead. In 1877 a trader called Easterbrook was also killed there. Two Royal Navy ships showed up demanding the handover of the guilty. The Tannese refused. In the meantime more missionaries – Neilson, Watt and Grey – had managed to gain a foothold, with no baptisms yet, but no murders either. The captain of the *Beagle* (not Charles Darwin's vessel) took seventeen natives hostage. Then the murderer, a man called Yuhmanga, turned up on the beach. He was told to step aboard the *Beagle*, but he refused, although he handed over his musket. Three men were dispatched to capture him, but he escaped. The search for the murderer resulted in the deaths of four Tannese, until they found Yuhmanga's brother. They decided that he would have to do, so they hanged him from the yardarm. But it was clear that the navy had better things to do with its time.

The missionaries plodded on, forever blaming the traders' activities for causing native hostility towards white men. This wasn't always unjustified. The Anglican Bishop Patteson was murdered in 1872, as a result of the previous incident, where blackbirders had invited locals on board to meet 'the Bishop'. But they'd thought there was something odd about Patteson from the start. Up in the north-east of the island chain, on Mota, ancestral memories tell of a mission-man by that name who took his shoes off and revealed that he had no toes. Man Mota hadn't seen socks before.

With levels of distrust so high, progress was slow. Missionary Neilson had spent eighteen years on Erromango without converting a single person. Nobody was baptised on Tanna until the 1880s. But the Christian incomers didn't help themselves by being such confirmed racists and sectarians. Doubts about the 'quality' of local converts meant there were few ordained priests who weren't white – in fact, there were no indigenous Roman Catholic priests until the end of World War Two.

Paton's publicity campaign brought funds, funds that meant hospitals and schooling, and eventually converts. The slow shift to Christianity was also partly due to a weakening of local defences. The whole sandalwood–blackbirding period had resulted in massive levels of depopulation. The population of Aneityum fell from 3500 in 1850 to 435 by 1905. That of Erromango had been 4500 before sandalwood; by 1930 it was less than 500. Illness was also to blame. 'We're not civilising them, we're syphillating them,' one Roman Catholic missionary commented.

The Presbyterians who targeted the southern part of the archipelago were an uncompromising lot, insisting on full-scale adoption of European ways and a total turning away from kastom. Villages were rebuilt along neat, Surrey lines. Traditional dances and kava were outlawed. The rich pageantry of the local ceremonial calendar was boiled down to the stultifying dullness of the Sabbath. It was this insistence, far more than the atrocities of the labour trade, which set the missionaries so firmly against the traders – who still offered the locals a means of improving their standard of living without dropping their identity. And it was this pious war on local values that in time sparked a kastom-led revolt on Tanna, under the banner of a new god.

I rejoined Yasu by the smouldering remains of the church, its dark, cracked beams reminding me of the Chief's shins, dried out from kava drinking.

'We burnt it last Wednesday,' he said, 'but it's still smoking.' He smiled at me dreamily. 'That's because Nakwa is very powerful. That church was part of his body and we destroyed it, but it could still burn you.'

'Why do you do everything on a Wednesday?'

'Don't listen to the Missionary,' he said darkly. 'We dance all the time. If there's a ceremony in a village, we go there to dance. We walk all day – even if it's on the other side of the island. We are free here.'

Yasu had been to New Caledonia, where he'd worked for a rich Frenchman, tending his horses. He felt sorry for that Frenchman, who was not free. Who had money, but had to work all day. Here on Tanna, he said, a man had his vegetable garden and plenty of wood and kava, and it was all he needed. 'No pem wan samting,' he said, fixing me with his unsettling, basilisk stare. You don't pay anything.

It was a mantra I'd heard often – and I wondered if it had some bearing on the Prince Philip cult. The Tannese loved their home as an adjunct of themselves, and pitied the rootless. Could they know the real Prince Philip had spent his boyhood being shunted from one relative to the next? That he loathed the chilly corridors of Buckingham Palace, and the skirling of the Scottish piper who woke the inhabitants at dawn? Did they know his cousin Alexandra, later Queen of Yugoslavia, remembered Philip as a boy, forever drawing sketches in the sand, of the house he would one day own. Was it pure coincidence that they'd imagined the Duke to be an exiled god?

The meeting had started to break up, and Yasu walked with me back down to the nakamal, along with the rest of the men. A giddy atmosphere had replaced the worshipful one of before, there was rib-nudging and laughter, and I suspected this might herald a midday dose of kava. My main concern was to avoid sitting next to the Missionary. But I had a stark choice to make. Undeterred by the constant gusts of wind, the locals obligingly lit half a dozen more of their speciality fires, so that the meeting ground began to ring with the sniffing and coughing and weeping of all who sat there.

'Why don't we build one big fire,' I suggested hopefully, 'over there, so the smoke blows in one direction, and we all get warm?'

With their eyes streaming and their voices strangled down to a whisper, the men informed me that this was impossible. 'We have never done that,' they croaked, outraged at the idea.

I was compelled to come out from among them and take my place upon a large log at the front, a point of safety in one regard, except that silently, with a cheesy smile, the Missionary now crept to join me there. Once everyone was settled, and the last child shooed away, Chief Jack rose to his feet and gave a generous oration, pointing first to the village, then to Nako, and then to me. Nako stood after that, and was received with a rustle of applause.

'Do you understand?' the Missionary hissed. 'I can speak Nauvhal.' Rather sheepishly, I admitted that I'd appreciate some help. 'The Chief says that everything before is forgotten. He has made Nako the Voice of the Canoe.'

'Voice of the Canoe' was a venerable title, an equivalent to the 'talking chiefs' of Samoa and Hawaii, or, to give it a modern spin, press officer for the village. It was a vivid demonstration of the Chief's faith in Nako, and seemed, from the gestures he had made, to be connected to me. But what had he meant about the past being forgotten? The Missionary said he didn't know.

It was time for Nako to make his maiden speech, a shorter affair than his father's, but including, I noticed, lavish reference to Prince Philip, his servant Big Ass Dear Summer Lance Daisies, and, most perplexingly of all, the Lovely Bungalows. The Missionary had no time to interpret, because our newly appointed Voice of the Canoe then summoned me, with just a touch of swagger, into the ring to read from the myths.

I opened my bag, and promptly discovered the myths had gone. This was puzzling, as I had a vivid memory of Siyaka using them, absent-mindedly, to burst open the body of a bothersome bluebottle, then guiltily wiping them on his hair. I'd stowed them in my bag after that, out of harm's way, and the whole thing had taken place just before sundown last night.

With a gleeful flourish Nako suddenly produced an off-white baton from his trouser pocket. 'I asked you if you had them,' he declared, with an air of the detective assembling key suspects in the drawing room, 'and you did said that you had them, but you did not have them!' He now unfurled his baton and revealed it to be my paperwork. I sensed he was hoping for a gasp from the crowd.

'You are not taking careful of them,' he continued. 'But they are very important to my father. So!' He held a finger aloft, and stepped out from the group to face me. 'From now on I will carry the stories with me, and when the people say, "Read us the stories," you will say, "Nako, give me the stories," and I will say, "Yes," and I will give the stories to you and you will read from the stories and then you will give them back to me and…'

'Nako – that's … that's a good idea,' I interrupted, dazzled by his capacity for repetition. He nodded fiercely and scanned the arena in case there should be any challenge. None came. 'Could I … erm … have them now?' I added.

Once the myths had been grudgingly delivered into my hands, I read the one about the man who'd heard Philip and the Queen talking on board the Royal Yacht *Britannia*. The audience seemed to enjoy it, but once again the mood was of a people politely receiving some fresh gospel.

'If the man was sitting on Blacksands Beach,' the Missionary offered, 'then he was probably from Imabel. That's the nearest village.'

He'd spoken cautiously, as if aware that he wasn't too welcome. But the group nodded and slapped the ground. The Chief, whose woolly halo and smoke-wreathed countenance lent him the look of some key player in the Greek myths, rose again and pointed at me. 'You must go to Imabel and speak to the men there,' he decreed. 'It must be one of them who spoke this story. I want to hear his voice.'

'So do I,' Nako added hastily. 'I am chief belong tok-tok. I order you to Imabel. And now read another one,' he said loftily. 'That one next about Philip's brothers.'

'Philip has many brothers,' I read. 'One of these brothers is John Frum, the man who came during World War Two and promised things to the people on the east of the island. Another is Jake Raites. Like John Frum, Jake Raites promised to help Tanna, but he went away to America. Today, all of America's power is because of that magic belonging to Jake Raites. He enables them to put men upon the face of the moon. America gives Jake Raites much money because of his strong magic.

'But money is something belonging to Nakwa. It is like the bush devils that call in the night and divert a

man returning home from the nakamal into danger.
Jake Raites has been seduced by Nakwa. That is why he
will not return to Tanna. Kalbaben is angry about this.
So he has given the work of John Frum and Jake Raites
to Prince Philip.'

I sat down, to a ripple of applause, to which the Missionary contributed just as enthusiastically as his pagan
brothers. I asked if anyone had heard the story before.
'Yes,' said Chief Jack helpfully. 'You read it out the
other day.'

'No, I mean…' I tried another angle. 'Who is Jake
Raites?' I asked, unable to disguise the faint catch of
desperation in my voice. 'Does anybody know who Jake
Raites is?'

'Well, it says in this letter that he is one of the brothers of Prince Philip,' said the Missionary, poring over
the pages in my hand. I snatched them away bad-tem-
peredly.

'I know what it says in the letter!' I snapped. 'And it's
not a letter! I just…' I stared over their heads at Mount
Tukosmwera, shimmering in the haze of the crackling
fires. I'd been told there were no human settlements
on its slopes, because it was a tabu place, nor any birds
or insects or pigs, because Kalbaben had commanded
them all to be silent. His mountain seemed now like
an impenetrable fortress: somewhere, on a high windy
ridge, were the secrets of the faith, but between us sat
miles of cultural scree and inscrutable villagers.

Now a small boy came belting along the main foot-path into the nakamal. I recognised him as belonging to our village – agitated, breathless and, so it seemed, drenched from head to foot, he addressed himself to the Chief. Most of the men shot to their feet, angry and shouting, and departed in the direction of Yaohnanen, among them Nako and Kal. The Chief himself rose painfully, and padded towards the exit, muttering all the while, and pausing, just for a moment, to cast an enigmatic look in my direction.

'What's happened?' I called out. The Chief mouthed something indistinct, and disappeared into the trees.

'It's a flood,' Yasu said.

'But it hasn't been raining.'

'No – in Yaohnanen they have a water tap. Somebody left it running, and all the gardens have been destroyed.'

He let his gaze linger on me for just a second longer, before drifting off into his own village. The other men followed suit, the meeting ruptured, and I was left alone in the place, with the wood smoke and spit and the breeze in the trees. Somebody left it running... And if I'd read Yasu's stare correctly, he didn't think it was just somebody.

I'd been the last man to use the tap. I'd swivelled it this way and that, trying to get water out, then left it. On? Or off? I hadn't bothered to check. The careless, clumsy act of a man too selfish to think of a tap's importance in this place.

Full of dread, I took the bush path back to the village. It would be wise, I knew, to make reparations – but what could I offer? Here – I imagined myself saying, to the fuming face of Kal – have this half-finished packet of Murray Mints. I hope that makes up for the total destruction of your livelihood.

'Well, well,' a voice exclaimed. 'The Englishman.'

I glanced up from my misery and saw a smooth, handsome individual smoking a corncob pipe by the brook. His tone of voice and his general demeanour suggested we'd had some appointment and I was late for it. He bade me sit with him, and so, in no hurry to return to the village, I agreed.

He was a slender creation of polished mahogany, with a neat woven pouch for his tobacco and a freshly ironed T-shirt picturing all the islands of the archipelago. His nostrils were aristocratically flared and that, plus the mahogany timbre of his voice, reminded me of the black British actor Don Warrington. He told me, in flawless English, that his name was Lomakom and he'd been one of the boys at the original kastom school. He'd become a teacher in Port Vila, but recently resigned.

'So what do you do now?'

'Gardening,' he said brightly. 'Did you enjoy the dancing?'

'Yes, I did.'

He tilted his head coquettishly. 'But you didn't come here to see Christians.'

I replied, carefully, that this was true. But that I wasn't sure what I'd seen today was very Christian, either.

'Oh yes it is, Matthew,' he said. I hadn't told him my name, so his use of it was a challenge. 'Unity is just a way of bringing the kastom people into Christianity. Did you meet the Missionary? Did you think him a very stupid man?' He didn't give me a chance to respond, before adding, 'He is not. He is hanging on, even though they burnt his church, because he knows one day they will all be Christians, and he can say it was his work. A jolly clever chap.'

I'd begun not to enjoy my chat with Lomakom. What I'd thought was natural courtesy turned out to be a mocking parody of my own manners. His smile was thin, and his eyes glinted like a pawnbroker's tooth. I felt as if I might be in the presence of Nakwa, the serpent god, himself. I stood up from the felled log we were sitting on, and shouldered my bag.

'Why are you going to Yaohnanen?' Lomakom purred. 'There is nothing for you there. Or anywhere on Tanna.'

'What do you mean?'

Lomakom smiled, the way Bond villains smile before opening trapdoors. 'Nobody knows anything about Prince Philip. It's dead.'

'But the Chief knows…'

'The Chief! Ha!' His voice dropped to a seductive murmur. 'Everyone is joining the Unity group

– that's why Nako came here today. Not to show you about Prince Philip. To see the Unity people, because his father is old, and even if Nako is stupid, he knows where the future is.'

A chill settled upon my shoulders. 'So why does everyone tell me they still believe?'

'They are lying,' he said, rising to stand with me. He put a light hand on my shoulder. 'You came for nothing, Matthew. Nothing at all.'

CHAPTER FOUR

In Which the Voice of the Canoe Explains to Me Full-up Times That I May Not Speak When He Is Not and Dysentery Proves My Undoing

A S I came down the slope from the tap next morning, my mind was on matters bodily rather than spiritual. 'Yu shit-shit wota,' had been Siyaka's cheerful observation last night, and he'd gone on to discuss this development vigorously with his fellows in the nakamal. A host of remedies had been suggested for the Englishman's unfortunate condition – more kava, more yams, and finally an odd, minty-tasting leaf, which I'd accepted but had made things many times worse. I'd started to wonder if they were poisoning me.

And so when I emerged, queasily, into the clearing where the hut stood, and found a number of unknown men squatting there, I wasn't surprised. They'd probably picked up, on the bush-email system, some fascinating rumours about this white man with a stomach complaint and were here to investigate.

'Lhua,' I greeted them. It meant 'good', and was, thus far, the only word of Nauvhal I'd mastered. They did not reply, but rose and stared. I shrugged, as if to say, 'What gives?', and a short, burly man, with the assumed importance of a site foreman, pushed himself forward. His T-shirt, rather unfortunately, said 'Candy Girl'.

'What is the name of your father?' he asked portentously.

'Anthony,' I said, before stepping into the hut for some more clothes. I heard them discussing this latest point heatedly. When I returned to the doorway I found them standing, stiff and proud, in orderly formation, as if for some missionary's photograph, circa 1900.

'We want to build a road,' announced the Foreman.

I sympathised. Despite the Chief's eulogies about Tanna's divinely constructed road network, transport on the island was in a shabby state. Most of its major roads were only passable by heavy-duty trucks, the purchase or rental of which was beyond the pockets of most people, especially the kastom folk.

'You need a lot of money for that,' I said.

There was much frowning and muttering, before the Foreman said, 'We want to build a road with you.'

A long silence followed while I took this in. What role did this deputation imagine me taking in their construction project? Stirring the tarmac? Or just handing over the funds? I supposed the word was out about me providing the tools for the kastom school, and perhaps people hoped I had money for other, equally worthy public works. 'I don't think I'll be here long enough to build a road,' I said.

The Foreman shot me an icy look. 'That's not the reason,' he spat. 'You only build roads with this village.'

The men about-faced and left, with a scattering of disgusted tribal clicks and hisses. Curled on the earth where they'd been standing was a battered leaflet for the Lovely Bungalows. Things were becoming very odd.

The previous afternoon I'd returned to the village with a spectrum of conflicting feelings. It had been a great relief to discover that I hadn't, in fact, flooded the yam gardens. There was another tap on the other side of the village, and this was the one that had been opened. The messenger boy had exaggerated his story, too, and only a part of one man's garden had been affected. But the easy routines of the nakamal had been disrupted. It was suspected that someone had turned that tap on, someone who wished harm to Yaohnanen, and the men had discussed it in tense whispers over the kava that night, even though Chief Jack had called for calm.

I hadn't joined in, or mentioned the strange, angry men who'd apparently tipped Nako into a bush. Because I found myself wishing a certain degree of harm upon Yaohnanen. With the lifting of my guilt over the tap, my fury was free to soar. Everything the sinister, serpent-like Lomakom had said made sense. It explained why they knew none of the Prince Philip myths, why there was no evidence of worship or prayer. My mission – visiting the outlying villages with my voice recorder – was a farce, one the Chief probably chuckled over as he lay down each night with his pet piglet. This was a community on the verge of going over to Christianity, but they wouldn't admit it while there was the potential of duping a foreigner.

I piled clothes into my holdall, with thoughts of making it down to the main road, and thence into Lenakel. I had no idea what I'd do there, of course, but I longed to be away from this tense, perplexing village. I rehearsed a curt but courteous farewell to the Chief, and was doing so when he materialised in front of me, like some aged genie from a drop of dew. He held a steaming slab of leaves and a book in his hands, and my surprise at seeing him there was so great that I jumped.

'What frightens you?' he asked. I told him I'd just been thinking about him when he appeared, and he said that was nothing to be afraid of. The old man squatted on the soil beside me and said there was a skin between this world and the nara wol, the realm of the supernatural. That kava could help men to pierce it, but only momentarily unless they were skilled magicians. That I had preconceived of his coming, because I had begun to take my first steps in this alternative dimension. It was a typical breakfast conversation as far as the Chief was concerned.

Then he handed me the slab of leaves and told me to unwrap it – the act of doing so revealing a grey cake of spongiform texture. 'Lap-lap,' the Chief said. 'It will be good for your belly.' Then he gave me the book – its pages spotted with mould and pitted with the drillings of long-dead insects. It was the book of his friend, Ken Dodd, he said. But it wasn't. It was a book by the absurdist actor-performer-writer Ken Campbell, who had, I knew, certain links to the South Pacific. I'd seen him on the news, doing *Hamlet* in pidgin. But what was the Ken Dodd connection?

'You can read it today,' the Chief said. 'You will have a lot of time, and you may get bored, so it will be good. But now…' He tapped the pages gently to get my attention. 'I want you to explain something. You are a writer of books, aren't you?'

'Yes, I am.'

'But if you are here on Tanna living with us, then who is writing the books? Does your father do it – or one of your brothers-in-law?'

'Erm… No. We have lots of people writing books all the time. Even Prince Philip writes books.'

The Chief's eyes widened. 'Give one of them to me.'

'I don't actually have one on me,' I said. 'But he's written lots of them. He wrote one called…' At this point, unfortunately, I could only remember the title of one book written by Prince Philip, and I suspected telling it to the Chief could lead us onto boggy ground. '*Competition Carriage Driving*,' I offered feebly.

The Chief mulled this over sagely. 'What does it mean?'

I took a weary breath. But at that moment Siyaka came lumbering across the little log bridge, slipping as he did so, grabbing a corner of the fence and bringing a fair portion of that down with him. Grinning goofily as he wiped mud from his skin-tight, once-white jeans, he said it was time to go.

'To Imabel?' I'd been promised a trip to this coastal village, where, according to myth, a man had heard Prince Philip breaking the Queen's heart on the decks of the Royal Yacht.

But Siyaka gestured vaguely into the sky. 'Not Imabel. Long way, Matthew. Up, down, up, down again – past the waterfall. A big, big ceremony in Iapnamal. Everybody dancing all night, lots of kava. We will have a lot of fun!' A collection of small, fidgety boys now appeared on the little track that ran parallel to the brook, shyly peeping at me through the trees and whispering. 'My boys,' Siyaka said, stabbing his chest, proudly. 'Very excited… What's the matter?'

He must have seen the emotions battling it out on my face. I was mystified and perplexed, angry and anxious, and 99 per cent certain that I'd been the victim of a tribal con trick. But it was impossible to stay angry in a place where, apparently without warning, everyone would down tools and head off to the mountains for an all-night party. Where an old Chief shuttled between discussing the supernatural and books for the bored, in the blink of a lizard's eye. This island, these people, deserved another chance.

'Nothing,' I said. 'Let's go.'

So we said our goodbyes to the old Chief and set out for Iapnamal, at the top of a distant valley. Siyaka carried a bulky radio with him, its aerial long since stripped to a coil of flex which, for better reception, he wound into the woolly kinks of his hair. The sound produced was like a massacre in a pet shop, with occasional, spectral traces of Celine Dion.

After an hour of gently undulating woodland paths, the trees thinned out and we came upon a chasm, split by a waterfall. Several major bush ways seemed to converge there, in a scene akin to the outskirts of a pop festival. Half of Tanna was on its way up to Iapnamal, laden with yams, man-sized heads of kava and steaming sheets of lap-lap. I'd passed my own helping, discreetly, to one of Siyaka's small boys, having discovered that lap-lap – a cake made of manioc flour and baked on hot stones – tasted just like yams, but a little worse. I thought it best to avoid food, in any case, given the fraught condition of my stomach.

But it didn't stop me being infected with the giddiness of the party crowd, who joked and passed sticks of tobacco up and down the phalanx like batons in a relay race. A cackling gang of teenage girls passed us, arms around each other's shoulders, and I felt wistful for the company of women, who seemed to occupy some sphere whose edges brushed only fleetingly against our own. There would be nods and laughs and playful slapping when the two sexes passed in the corridors of the bush, but that was its limit.

I'd heard of a Chief in one village who'd been hauled up by the government for destroying the water tap they'd issued. Unrepentant, he said he'd done it because it was the job of the women to fetch water. This they'd done each day with the girls, a task taking around three hours, leaving the men in the nakamal with the boys. Suddenly, with the tap installed, everyone was bumping into each other. People started criticising each other's child-rearing, there were rows, and, inevitably, illicit liaisons in the bush. So the Chief had shoved a stick up the spout and covered the tap with a namwele leaf, rendering it tabu.

But women weren't exactly tabu themselves, and if I was truly to understand the island's ways, it was a mistake to speak to only half of its population. Perhaps they were all misleading me, but the more people I spoke to, the more I'd know. And I had a perfect line of enquiry already waiting for me.

'Siyaka,' I asked, as we hopped in front of the waterfall along a line of boulders, 'can I talk to some women?'

'You want women?' he asked doubtfully.

'No, I mean I...'

A youth with an almost vertical shock of hair walked by and nudged Siyaka. 'What does he want?'

'Women,' Siyaka replied. The shock-headed fellow appraised me through narrowed eyes.

'Why didn't you bring your wife?'

He clicked his teeth and scrambled on ahead. We started to power our way up a steep, slippery hill, holding onto slender saplings to prevent a fall. I tried again.

'No, Siyaka, I want to talk to the three virgins who were going to be given as brides to Prince Philip.'

'Three virgins?'

'Yes. I want to know if they're still virgins.' Siyaka shot me a horrified glance. 'I mean, what happened to them? Did they ever get married? Have they had to stay single, in case Prince Philip comes?'

We paused, clinging to creepers and branches on the impossible, mocking slopes, while the boys just scrambled ahead like little tanks in T-shirts. 'You want us to send three of our girls to Prince Philip,' Siyaka mused. 'I think it will be possible. But you should talk to the Chief about it.'

With a grunt he headed on up, his broad bare back glistening with sweat. I shook my head, stumped again.

Did he have no memory of the three-virgins offer? Or was he just being evasive?

I came over the slope and into a small, fly-blown nakamal with a skew-whiff shelter in one corner. Yaohnanen's meeting place, in keeping with its status, was scruffy but dramatic, its ring of banyan trees like the vaulted lid of some living cathedral. This one was just desolate, though, its central banyan mottled with some vivid type of tree pox, the arena strewn with shards of reed and twists of rope and rubbish. The boys chased an animal into the bush. Siyaka called me over to the shelter.

Within its draughty walls I discovered a scene recalling some bucolic painting of English rural life. A long figure, obscured by sacking cloth, snored theatrically in the corner. Two others sat on mud in a fog of kava. One had the blinking, rabbity look of a country parson, the other, beetle-browed, aggrieved and fat, suggested a squire with debts, an effect underlined by his wearing two-thirds of an old tweed jacket.

'Tuk Noao is buried here,' Siyaka said. 'Just down the hill. This man – his kin,' he added, pointing to the fat man. We all shook hands. The snoring in the corner grew louder.

'So you are the man who will steal the feather of Yakel and return it to Yaohnanen,' said the Parson. I asked what he meant. He gave a cautious smile and the tubby Squire blew air through his lips in a long, defeated sigh. 'Ask your Chief,' the Parson added mildly, taking up a piece of coconut and rubbing it into his kava-cracked limbs.

'Matthew... Would you, er, like some, er...?' Siyaka asked hopefully, miming the downing of a kava shell's contents. I shook my head. An encounter with a kinsman of Tuk Noao, a founding father of Philippism, could not be thrown away in silent hallucination. He too was rolling a piece of coconut shell over and over in his fingers, and in doing so, despite the double chin and overwhelming air of defeat, he brought back memories of his ancestor's appearance in the film I'd seen all those years ago in Cambridge.

When I'd first learned of the Philip cult's existence, Tuk had been flipping a British coin in his hand, its alloyed metals, silver and brown, providing the starting point for an impressive discourse. The silver, he explained, was the white man, the brown, the black man – the coin, with its image of Queen Elizabeth, symbolised the eventual harmony of black and white. Tuk's right hand, he said, was kastom, his black side. His left hand belonged to the white side, and he loved and needed them both, just as a man does his hands.

Another pole of Philippist thought fell into place now, like the beams of a slowly forming log house. Whenever I'd read the myths to people, there'd been a lot of concern about left and right. Queen Elizabeth was made, in the narrative, to stand on Prince Philip's left side – his white side –while the right, black side of him faced the land of his birth. It tied into this wider theme of men and islands all possessing some other half from which they'd been separated. It also suggested Tuk Noao might have been the source of at least one of the myths. But why wouldn't Chief Jack, his friend and co-visionary, have known it, too?

'I came to Tanna,' I said, 'because I was interested in some of the things Tuk said.'

The Squire nodded roughly and asked to look at my watch. He inspected it, and returned it to me wordlessly. The rasping snores of the man in the corner now reached pneumatic drill levels, but nobody else paid any mind.

'Tuk was clever,' said the Parson, trying to compensate for his friend's behaviour. 'One time, he dreamt about a pigeon...'

'No!' interrupted the Squire irritably. 'He *met* a pigeon. And the pigeon told him she would give him a vision in a dream.'

'Ah, that's true,' conceded the Parson affably, as if he'd been corrected on the scores in a recent cricket match. 'Anyway, Tuk went to sleep and the pigeon came into his dream and she told him you would be coming.'

'Me?'

'Well, no, white men, tourists...' the Parson elaborated. 'So when he woke up, Tuk told everyone this would happen. He got all the kastom people together and told them to be ready for the white men. To make dances. Show them how we live.'

But Tuk's proto-tourism movement had had its detractors, it seemed. 'One village was afraid the white men would be like the white men who came before,' said the Squire, unexpectedly joining in. 'So they built a big fence, so nobody could see inside their village. Another village said John Frum was the only white man they wanted to see. But another village, well, they took hold of the idea like a child with his father's hand.'

'What village was that?'

'What do you think?' snapped the Squire. He winced as he shifted position, and I realised his dull eyes and moody expression were the result of great pain. The heel of his right foot was split in two, the lower half revealing a jam-like mess underneath. I asked how he'd done it. 'Dancing,' he replied vaguely. 'Early in the morning, near to your village. That's the village I'm talking about.'

'Yaohnanen?' I was puzzled. Apart from the odd hack on the scent of Philippism, the place they called my village seemed perpetually ignored by the tourist trail.

'Yes, because Chief Naiva trusted the dream. Back in those days Yaohnanen was where all the whites came with their cameras. The name of it means "I see a stranger." So the strangers came, not to Yakel, but to your village.'

'But not now,' I prompted.

The Squire and the Parson exchanged looks. 'No. Because...'

Siyaka embarked upon a bout of loud and, to my mind, artificial coughing, which put the men off their stride. At the same time Nako entered the village, swaying like a tugboat in a strong current, on his back a shirt patterned with purple parrots.

'Where've you been?' I asked. He met this with a scowl, and said some gruff things to Siyaka, before telling me it was time to go.

Something odd occurred at that point. While I was focusing on Nako, I was aware of movement in the shelter behind me, of people standing up and shifting around. The next thing I knew, a man in suspiciously neat clothes had showed up. 'Hello, Matthew,' he purred. 'What a surprise to see you here.'

I looked round in confusion. Where had he sprung from? The sack pile was still there. It was not, however, making any snoring noises.

'Lomakom,' I replied tightly. 'Been asleep, have you?'

He frowned. Perhaps I was wrong. 'I need a sleep,' he replied with a glistening smile. 'I was dancing, very early this morning. I'm very tired.'

Some tight words were traded between Nako and Lomakom, petering out into short, fierce, upward nods

of the head and flashing looks. They reminded me of
two boys I'd seen in a Sydney bar, coming to blows over
the pool table. I wanted to see more, but I was ush-
ered away and marched to the next hill, where Nako
stood me against a lone coconut palm and asked me
how it was that Lomakom knew my name. I explained
about our conversation as Nako's face grew ever more
pinched with fury.

'He is one of the enemy of my father,' he spat. 'One
of the people against him.'

'I didn't know that. He just said he did gardening.'
And dancing, I remembered. Sometimes Tannese life
sounded rather like the diaries of the Mitford sisters.

'Not gardening,' Siyaka said, more gently. 'He belongs to politik, Matthew. Vanuaaku Pati. Bad man.'

'You will not speak any words among the people
when I am not,' Nako thundered. 'You do not understand how it is our way. You will not ask the questions
about the Prince Philip any more now. If you want to
ask it, you ask just me.'

And we walked on in silence. Siyaka flashed me a
sympathetic look, an act which took his eyes off the
path long enough for him to career down a short gully,
snag his eighties disco trousers on a thorn bush and
drop his ancient ghetto blaster in a heap of liquid shit.
But none of that made me smile. I was furious about
Nako's gagging order, and what it might mean. Why
was Nako so concerned to police me?

I was also bothered by the mention of Yakel in my recent conversation with the men. For I had business there, business that might be difficult to carry out. In Sydney, Kirk Huffman had given me a pair of thick reading glasses, requested by an old friend of his, Johnson Kowiya, Chief of Yakel. I'd arrived on Tanna determined to take them to him, but then various comments from Chief Jack and others had indicated some obscure and ancient quarrel between the two villages. I'd kept quiet, and almost let the matter slip from my mind. But I owed it to Kirk to do it – he'd welcomed me into his home, lent me books and documents, asking in return only this small, potentially interesting task of me. The spectacles would need to be handed over. But I might not mention it just now.

We came at last upon a high, flat plain, flecked with moist nuggets of goat shit and crowded with celebrants from all across the island. Men and women had decked themselves out with face paint, and garlands of tinsel, yams, kava, pigs and slabs of the joyless lap-lap were stacked all around. People set up camp in precise patterns, linked, so Siyaka said, to the location of their home villages, and the air was charged with the squealing of pigs. It was a cross between some ancient pagan rite, a pop festival and a country show, and we'd arrived at a crucial moment.

A long line of small boys – eight or nine years old, plastered in make-up – were led out of the bush and walked around a ring like show cattle. 'They have been in the bush with their grandfathers,' Siyaka said. The phrase reminded me of what Chief Jack had said when I'd asked about the ghostly music in the trees. 'They are cut, then they stay in the bush a long time,' Siyaka elaborated. 'They go to the sea to wash every day, and nobody must see them. So they blow shells to make people know they are coming.'

So that explained the Mystical Youth Orchestra – it was a choir of the circumcised, on their way to bathe in salt water. The thought was a painful one, and I noticed some trace of historic discomfort in Siyaka's face, too. He gazed fondly at one of his own lads, too small for the snip just yet, and currently chasing a butterfly with a twig. 'What do the boys do in the bush?'

'Learn secret things,' Siyaka said, with an apologetic shrug. In some parts of the archipelago, I knew, the elders banged on the doors of the boys' bush lodge in the night, claiming to be ghosts who wanted sexual intercourse with them. The initiates might also be starved and fed rotting food, beaten and deliberately bewildered. A process – very like school and military service – designed to drum society's sterner values into sullen heads.

A stultifying bolt of kava was administered to me at that point, and then I watched a bewildering sort of ballet, in which the men of various villages handed great piles of vegetables and kava to each other, while a legion of prize-winning hogs noisily met their deaths in the background. 'You see, there, Matthew,' Siyaka rumbled, doing his best to provide a commentary while entirely poleaxed on kava. 'The men of Ioknaauka swap with Iekwatengteng, see? Now ... this is Iakukak, I think ... no, no, it's Ielgis, yes, the men of Ielgis swapping with the men of Imanaki...'

There was a strict order for it all – each village swapping only with certain others, and further villages occasionally serving as intermediaries. The pidgin term for it was 'swappem'. Swappem – or rather the neglect of it – had lain behind the villagers' feelings of annoyance when Alexander Wilkie failed to reciprocate the gift of a pig from Yaohnanen back in 1966. In fairness to Mr Wilkie, he did die that same year. But had the villagers not demanded some recompense for the perceived slight, the world might never have known of their most startling beliefs.

Swappem was unique to Tanna. Up on Malekula island, to the north, they preferred a ferocious kind of proto-capitalism. Society was ordered into a lengthy ladder of grades, called nimangki, the men at its pinnacle regarded as so sacred and dangerous that they were treated as if already dead. To become a 'Big Man' and gain entrance to the VIP lounge of Melanesian village society, you must obtain, nurture and ultimately give away valuable pigs to those in the grade above. Existence, for Man Malekula, was a lifelong version of

The Apprentice – a vigorous fray of intrigues and faction fights. Down Tanna way they preferred an equilibrium, even if chasing it necessitated a permanent state of riot. If one village gave a mighty shipment of produce to another, then it had to be returned, yam for yam. To give less would be mean. To give more would be vulgar.

Moving Food Around is a very Pacific preoccupation, an answer to the problem of what to do with all the produce. There's not a lot of specialisation in these village societies. There are a few professionals – chaps who know the magic for making huge bananas, or whistling up a rain storm. But for the most part, each fellow tends his own garden and, thanks to richly fertile soils, you'd have to try damned hard not to acquire a stonking great surplus of yams, manioc, taro and kava. But this is stuff that rots – it can't be stored indefinitely – and so people prefer to use it as a political tool. Whether you swap it to keep the peace, or try to boost your status with displays of generosity, the shuffling of grub is wrapped up with relations between individuals and groups. There's no such thing as a free lunch in Melanesia.

The swappem cycle held a great fascination for Siyaka and his chums, sinking a further round of murky kava shells as barrowloads of local produce were shuttled from one part of the field to another. With the exception of Nako, whose sullen intoxication reminded me of Glaswegians on late-night trains, the men were a friendly bunch. They were animated when discussing Tanna's thirty-two different kinds of yam and the perplexing lack of lap-lap in London, sheepish if any other subject reared its head. I must have looked bored and Nako caught it, and I, for my part, also caught the glinting smile that this raised in him. It was what he wanted, I realised – me, at his side, dosed into compliance on kava, trapped in a circle discussing yams, discovering nothing.

A pouty, moist-eyed teenager in a camouflage T-shirt came across and spoke to the men. Heads turned my way. Nako's thin smile disappeared. 'He is a boy of Chief Kowiya,' he slurred at me through frozen lips. 'Kowiya is at this place and he did send him sideways across the place at us.'

'Yes?'

'The Chief Kowiya says you have one something,' Nako said, in an accusatory tone, 'to give into his hands from the Cook Gavman.'

So Kowiya knew about the spectacles already – alerted through the bush-email system linking Kirk's flat in Bondi to the myriad islands of the Pacific. 'It's just some glasses,' I said lightly. 'Perhaps I could give them to him now.' I'd suddenly glimpsed a delightful escape route from Nako's vegetable circle, but the surly Voice of the Canoe shook his head with slow satisfaction.

'You cannot do here,' he said, bitterness co-mingling with joy. 'It must be done in our way.' He spat on the floor and added, 'Because this is the island of us.'

I held Nako's gaze for just a second longer than was polite, then looked disdainfully at the trees. A new cohort of men joined us then, fresh from the swap-pem fray, their biceps garlanded with golden seaweed. And at the same time a large, grey pig, on the brink of having its skull caved in with a club, made a noisy dash for freedom just a few feet away, pursued by angry men and delighted boys. So great was this diversion that I, still smarting with anger, sprang up and walked away. Nobody noticed, no one came after me. I was, for the moment, free.

So I did a circuit of the festive field, being called over by at least four different villages to hear about the heroic qualities of Tannese yams and tell people my father's name. During the last of these encounters my stomach began to boil with angry gases, finally produc-ing such an almighty, resounding fart that conversation all around gave way to shock and awe.

Some helpful individuals directed me to a bush toilet – a refreshingly sturdy construction behind a screen of reeds, where I found some vague relief. But I was shivering when I came out, so I sat in the sunlight and thumbed weakly through the book Chief Jack had given me. The hairy pig, I noticed vaguely, was still run-ning for its life.

It seemed Ken Campbell had visited Yaohnanen, dressed as, and claiming to be, the Scouse mirth-maker Ken Dodd. There was no reason for this, other than it being wacky and absurd and the sort of thing Ken Campbell went in for. There was no point being po-faced about Philippism – many aspects of it made me smile – but I didn't share Ken Campbell's view that the people of Tanna were simple fodder for a stand-up routine. It saddened me that the Chief had called him a friend, because the book contained a great many unfriendly things about him and his island.

I was about to put it back in my bag, when I noticed a line that made me think about Jake Raites, ne-er-do-well brother to Prince Philip and John Frum. In Ken Campbell's account a figure called 'Jack Karatis' was identified to him as being Jesus Christ.

'Jake Raites,' I said quietly, then 'Jesus Christ' and 'Jack Karatis', testing out the words, just as the Tannese did whenever I told them my dad's name. It was quite possible. Understandings on Tanna came about so often like this – like the slow filtration of rainwater through rock. And nowhere did this happen more than in the realm of language. It was the white man's desire to trade in sea-slugs – known by the French as bêche-de-mer – that had first necessitated the invention of a lingua franca pidgin, and Bislama, pronounced *BISH-la-ma*, became its name. The word is a pidgin form of 'Beach-La-Mer', itself a corruption of 'bêche-de-mer'. And so many of Bislama's terms sounded utterly foreign, until they'd been in my mouth long enough to lose the unfamiliar tang of Tanna. 'Like', for instance, was 'olsem' – from 'all a same'. 'What' was 'wanem' – 'what name'. And 'just' – I liked this best – was rendered in Bislama as 'nomo', which for me always evoked the scene of some hard-bitten sea-slug buyer bargaining down to just a shilling, no more.

'Jake Raites,' I repeated. 'Jack Karatis. Jesus Christ.' It was a simple language, encrusted with Melanesian habits of pronunciation, designed for commerce and work. Western visitors were tickled by terms like 'rubba belong fak-fak' for 'condom' and 'bugarup' for 'broken'. Then there was the Olympian 'bilak-bokis-we-i-gat-bilak-tut-mo-i-gat-waet–tut-sipos-yu-kilim-em-i-sing-aot', which ensured nobody in the archipelago would ever bother referring to a piano, let alone shipping one in. But I often wondered if the stripped-down concepts of Bislama contributed to the disdainful Western view of the people who used it. Their language sounded charming, but daft, child-like even – just like the Prince Philip cult. No wonder people had trouble taking it seriously.

'Jake Raites,' I said again, as at the muddy fringes of the field five of Tanna's burliest food-swappers aimed flying tackles at the fugitive hog.

'Is the brother of John Frum and Prince Philip,' said a voice to my left. I glanced up and found that the shock-headed young man, the one who'd passed us earlier on the path, was seated on a nearby log, chewing bright-pink bubblegum.

'And Jake Raites is Jesus?' I asked tentatively.

'Could be,' said the lad, blowing a bubble. His skin was so black it was almost blue, and this, combined with the startling hairdo, gave him the look of one electrified by spirit. The remainder of him, though, was pure Neasden High Road, circa 1990: a short green bomber jacket, baggy red tracksuit bottoms with gang-graffiti adorning each leg.

'We've got this one story says Philip wants to leave the mountain, to join the war,' the lad continued, in easy, Australian-accented English. 'Begs his dad three times. But his dad won't let him. Kalbaben says something like, "No. Who'll make kava when you're buggering about in the war?" So Philip stays, but he's thinking about the world below the mountain, y'know, and feeling sad. And Kalbaben, he's calling all the time for him to come and chew the kava and Philip can't hear because he's sad. And Kalbaben gets angry. And he calls until his voice cracks right up and the sun's nearly set before Philip comes over.' The young bloke left his log now and came to squat next to me. 'And Philip says, "You let my brother John Frum go to America. You got to let me go." See, that's how Kalbaben realised he's got to let Philip go. So he gives him a white horse, and off he goes to the war.'

It was a pretty verbatim version of one of the myths I'd brought with me, and evidence, surely, that Philippism flourished, even in the hearts of hip-hop fans. The detail about Philip going to war was new, though. Men like Chief Naiva and Tuk Noao must have been in that situation – begging the elders for permission to go and help the Americans. So whoever had dreamt up that version of events must have seen Prince Philip as an equal of his own generation. And perhaps he also knew a little history. In the opening years of the conflict known on Tanna as Wolwatu, the mortal Prince of Greece was champing at the bit out in Ceylon, begging his surrogate dad, Louis Mountbatten, for a chance to get dirty. But Greece hadn't entered the conflict. Only once Philip's country had been invaded could he come back to Europe, guns a-blazing, for his glorious war.

'That's why kastom people don't go with Jesus,' the lad said. Others had begun to cluster around us now, a welcome diversion, perhaps, from the interminable game of swappem on centre court. 'See, Jesus – Jake they call him – promised to help Tanna, but then he goes off to America, and he gives them his magic, and they give him money, so he forgets about helping Tanna, same as John did.'

'John Frum?'

He gave me a bashful grin. 'S'what the story says, anyway.' I got the sense that this young buck prayed in the direction of Brooklyn more than Buckingham Palace, but he'd helped me to understand the stories more clearly. The Jake Raites idea accounted for the kastom people's rejection of Christianity and

John Frum, and the ascendancy of the Philip cult. The promises made by Jesus and John Frum had not been fulfilled. It was said that they had become lost, seduced by the things of this world. If that was true, then Philippism wasn't an offshoot of John Frum: it was more of a revolt against it. I realised I didn't really know enough about this other, strange, Stars and Stripes-worshipping movement to be sure, and I needed to.

My informant's name was Daniel, and he worked in Port Vila, but was back visiting relations on Tanna. They lived in a little village on the coast.

'What's its name?' I asked. 'Perhaps I could come and visit?'

'Why not?' he said agreeably. 'I'm there next week. It's called Imabel.'

'Imabel?'

I'd already had his village down as the most likely source for the story about the Royal Yacht. And if Daniel knew all these other stories, the ones so strange and surprising to the men in Yaohnanen, perhaps his village, Imabel, had an alternative Philip cult going. This could be the vital clue.

'I don't suppose...'

But my words were interrupted by a roar of dismay. Nako came lurching across the field, scattering party-goers, goats and mandarin peel in his wake. Siyaka scuttled behind, blearily anxious.

'I explained to you full-up times you may not speak when I am not!' Nako thundered. 'I am Voice of the Canoe!'

'I don't care who you are,' I replied roughly. 'Don't shout at me.'

I sensed the silent, breathless crowd. Nako put his fingers in a belt loop of Siyaka's muddy jeans and dragged him over to me. 'Siyaka will stay at the side of you all the time. So that if I am not here, you will not be alone.'

'No,' I said. 'Sorry, Siyaka. But I don't need a guard. I'm here to do a job. And I need to ask questions of people, all the time. My own questions.'

Nako glared up into my face. His eyes looked like a pair of curdled puddings. 'You cannot ask the questions of you,' he rasped, blasting the clinical odour of freshly chewed kava into my nostrils. 'This is not your island. You don't recognise how it is our way.'

'Go on then,' I snapped. 'Explain it. Tell me how it is your way. Go on.'

Nako was still glaring at me. 'And one another thing,' he grated. 'You may not ask Siyaka questions about the three girls which was sending for the wives of the Prince Philip. You may not speak this to anybody.'

'Anything else?' I fumed. 'What questions am I allowed to ask, Nako? How are the yams? Do you have kava in England?' I stalked away, steaming with anger. A loutish bark from Nako summoned me back, but I kept on walking. I walked past the piles of produce, past the last of the doomed pigs, past the painted women and the playing children, back onto the high, draughty plain far above the sea, speckled with sparse fruit trees. And I sat under one, ashamed but defiant, blowing the fury out of me in hard, deliberate breaths, as the sky turned from blue to brown, and the festival resumed its rhythms. We're always angriest with someone when some little part of us knows we've been at fault, too. And perhaps I was at fault, failing to understand or even trying to understand, what Nako's problem was, why he couldn't let me wander the island, talking to whomsoever I wanted.

I took my little potted history of Vanuatu out of my bag, and read to calm myself. It only intensified my uneasiness, though, as I realised that I was merely the last in a long line of rude Europeans who've ridden roughshod over local sensitivities.

'Dogs and niggers are forbidden to enter inside the portals of these gates,' read a notice outside an early-twentieth-century Englishman's plantation on the island of Aore. 'Any dogs or niggers found therein will suffer the penalty of death.' It wasn't clear how either group was supposed to read it.

As sandalwood and human labour started to yield less profit, the Europeans turned to the coconut. Its dried flesh, copra, was a valuable source of crude oil, and could be used for soap. In the 1880s both British and French formed their own copra conglomerates, acquiring land and settling close by. Fights were frequent. The hotel in Port Vila was called 'the bloodhouse', because of the near-nightly murders that graced its veranda. Sometimes there were pitched gun battles between the British and French, such as at Port Sandwich, on Malekula, in 1888. That one, to the disappointment of all, had no fatalities, chiefly because it was Christmas and everyone was too drunk to shoot straight.

For years the two countries' governments wrangled over a permanent means of solving all these disputes, while the chattering classes of London and Paris were alerted, by eloquent missionaries, to the un-Christian excesses of the traders and planters. In the end, like a couple dazzled each other's stubbornness, the two governments entered into marriage. The Condominium of the New Hebrides was formed in 1906.

For the first three years the Condominium had no court. When it finally arrived, justice had its wings rather clipped by the fact that the British and French judges could not understand one another. In addition, the whole affair was presided over by the King of Spain, who spoke neither language and was also profoundly deaf. The Joint Court could neither arrest nor enforce. Its main function was fining people for selling alcohol to the natives. One trader, after kidnapping several people from the island of Santo, was alleged to have shot an escapee in the head with his revolver. Brought before the court, he was fined £20 and given a month in jail.

One enterprising French planter on Santo exploited the fact that his own vessel looked very like the one that belonged to the joint government. In 1911 he sailed to Malekula dressed in military gear and threw sticks of dynamite into the sea. Locals swarmed out to collect the dead fish – and were promptly arrested by the planter. For their 'crime', they were given three years' hard labour, unsurprisingly to be carried out on his own plantation. For his crime, the planter received no penalty at all. Those who did get jailed could choose between the British and the French jail. The food in the latter was, of course, superior, but there was said to be a greater risk of buggery.

An embarrassment to both governments, the Condominium, or 'Pandemonium' as residents dubbed it, was perfect material for an Ealing Comedy. Expats swear each administration sent out a man with a tape measure every day, to check the British and French flags were flying at the same height. Serious matters were referred back to Europe, and it often took a year for a decision to be reached. Both administrations were supposed to patrol the territory at regular intervals. But the British government's yacht, the *Euphrosyne*, caught fire, so they had to borrow the French one, when it was available and the French felt generous. Collecting customs revenues was a hoot, with two currencies and two sets of weights and measures.

Efforts were made to strengthen the standard of government in 1914 – but, owing to the war, nothing was done until 1922. Meanwhile questions were asked in the House. In 1921 it was suggested in Parliament that we hand the lot over to France in exchange for some territory elsewhere. It was decided instead to continue with the proud British tradition of grumbling but doing nothing. By 1934 the Condominium was costing us £23,362 and yielding just £10,719.

With government so sketchy, on many islands it was the missionaries, bolstered by alliances with local Big Men, who really held the power. This was the case on Tanna, where Frank Paton, son of the mellifluous John G., established himself in 1896. Frank won support from two prominent local men, Yawis and Lomai. He pursued a clever policy of employing locals in exchange for money and then gradually introducing prayer and religious instruction into the working day.

By 1870 most Europeans on Tanna were making their living from copra, trading merchandise in exchange for coconuts and labour from the villagers. They also started using Tannese men to purchase the copra on their behalf, meaning that some people were opting out of the traditional swappem economy. The missionaries themselves were caught up in this – selling the copra of people who converted, but not those who remained heathen – and became a rival business force to the traders, who offered locals a means of earning cash without turning Christian.

But not all missionary activity was malignant. Frank Paton bravely went into troubled areas, risking death in order to bring peace. He also helped those who lived in turbulent regions to settle within the safe confines of Christian villages. It came at a price, though. Paton was vigorously opposed to paganism, and outlawed the bulk of kastom beliefs. Kava could no longer be drunk or exchanged. He conducted forays into pagan villages, to capture the magic stones of the sorcerers.

But he couldn't abolish the old beliefs. With the traditional sorcerers deprived of their essential tool kit, a new and more malevolent form of magic, su, took hold. It's said that su came from outside – allegedly given by Ambrym men to the Tannese when both were working copra plantations on the island of Efate. Various objects were sold to would-be Tannese magicians, including small stones which are believed to have been made by mixing the hair, nails and brain of a dead man.

Su was a source of chaos in a way that traditional sorcery was not. The village sorcerer was part of the furniture, the local GP almost, whose prescription pad gave him access to the spirit world. But possessors of su magic stayed in the shadows, using their skills to cause illness and death to personal enemies. As mainstream, legitimate sorcery was undermined by the mission, the new magic caused paranoia and suspicion within villages and families. Others claimed to be witch-finders, with the skill to sniff out and expose su practitioners. And some used this 'skill' as a means of settling scores for others – accusing the man who'd got the girl you wanted, or the man to whose land you believed you were entitled, of using su.

Frank Paton thought he'd been astute in delegating so much power to local Big Men, who flexed their muscles through their role as Assessors in the Native Courts. But he underestimated the vigour Man Tanna applies to matters political. When Yawis and Lomai organised the resettlement of people from war-torn areas near to the calmer Christian villages, they spied an opportunity for score-settling. They ensured refugees were placed on the lands of their enemies, who lost the right to use them. Disputes begun in that time were still rattling on in the 1950s.

From 1896 to the 1940s, a period known as 'Tanna Law' ensued, still spoken of with dread today. It was a theocracy: government by the mission, backed up by the Christian Big Men. People were sentenced to hard labour for missing church, working on the Sabbath, dancing, using kava, even eating with their hands. There was three months' jail for bathing in the sea on a Sunday, and nastier cases of people being whipped, tied up and forced to eat excrement. Christians got off lightly; heathens faced the harshest sentences. There was no prosecution and no defence. There had, it was discovered, been only one acquittal in six years. Without kava no important ceremonies could take place. Kastom was slowly strangled.

But the Tannese did not suffer in silence. In 1908 and 1909 they used Humes and Truss, two sympathetic British traders, to take messages to the government in Port Vila, complaining about mission activities. The local pagans wanted to know, was it right that they should be forced to go to church? Why should the word of Christians affect people in non-Christian villages? They complained that kava plants had been uprooted. That the missionary Nicholson had intercepted, and withheld, a letter from the British government addressed to a Man Tanna.

The complaints of the Tannese were heard. In 1911 the bungling forces of the Condominium government managed to co-ordinate for a brief, inspired interlude. It was agreed that a delegate, or District Agent, would be placed on Tanna. Enter Mr Wilkes.

Wilkes overhauled the Native Courts. The District Agent would now preside over all court proceedings. There would be a fair balance of Christian and pagan judges, applying penalties strictly codified, in proportion to the offence. Wilkes followed this up in 1914 by allowing kava and dancing in the name of the Condominium government.

But he had a formidable opponent in the missionary Dr Nicholson. They'd almost come to blows when

Nicholson forbade Christians to meet with a delegation from a French warship which had come to sort out a dispute. Pagans had tried to approach the coast, but Nicholson, on horseback, had prevented them. When Wilkes intervened, the man of God responded that he would shoot the first French sailor who set foot on shore. The warship sloped off. Wilkes wrote a report about Nicholson's activities, which his subject caught sight of. He responded by writing an insulting letter forbidding Wilkes to go near his house. The government ordered Nicholson to apologise, but he never did.

Finally, the trenches of Flanders seemed a more easygoing place than Tanna, and Wilkes left his position for a commission in the army. He was replaced by Mr James M. Nichol, a Scottish engineer who'd formerly been in charge of the maintenance of the British government's yacht. The one that burnt to a cinder. You could hardly conceive of a man less equipped to deal with the period ahead.

I shut my book wearily, viewing the period immediately ahead of me with resignation. I was a solitary white man, attending a mountain-top ritual on a South Pacific island. It wasn't the place to go making livid speeches, cutting remarks or brave stands. It was my job to go back to the crowd, find Nako, apologise and accept his own kind of Tanna law. I stood up, an action coinciding with the moment my broiling guts converted, in their entirety, to water. Sharp pains shot up my back, the foul taste of Venice in a heatwave rose in my throat. Fittingly, at that moment the now-black sky burst open with a cosmic rip.

Within seconds I was sliding around in a bog. A thick mist descended with the speed of a drop hammer, but I knew where the ceremonies were, so I boldly struck out, each stride a struggle with the sucking mud. Inexplicably, as if some spiteful god had flipped the landscape thirty degrees, I found myself heading downhill, faster and faster, and finally sliding towards a sheer drop. I grabbed a bush and held on with bleeding hands as the rain hammered my scalp and lightning skewered the sky. 'Oh shit,' I said, with feeling.

A shape appeared through the swirling mist – I noticed its large ears first, then nothing else for a while. 'Matthew,' it called. 'Matthew.' Was it Prince Philip, come in spirit form to rescue me? Then it reappeared and I saw a bare chest, a pair of squelching trousers. 'Matthew. Where are you?'

Meekly I called out, and allowed Siyaka to haul me up the slope and lead me back to the field where the people where cowering from the sudden storm. It was a bad ceremony, people were saying. Someone had made it rain. There was ill feeling, quarrels all over the place, and people falling sick.

CHAPTER FIVE

In Which a Sorcerer Finds My Spectacles

AND the rain continued to thunder down like the horsemen of some pitiless army, turning the festival field into a delta and driving all those with no kin in the village into a gnarled old cow shed smaller than my first bedsit. I lay on damp reed mats, drenched and sick, between Siyaka and a powerfully scented gentleman in a Manchester City shirt, all of us packed so tight that to scratch one's balls required the cooperation of a dozen others.

'We have many kinds of yams on Tanna *pphwt*,' the strong-smelling man intoned happily in between bursts of championship spitting, 'a purple kind and a hairy kind and *pphwt* a woman yam and a man yam and a yam that's almost as tall as you *pphwt*...' I nodded weakly, barely taking part in the world around me. The air was thick with the fumes of the kerosene and the slathered-on face paint of the women, who were confined to the other half of the shelter, screened from our view by a hasty arrangement of rice sacks. I was dying.

'Very bad,' Siyaka said glumly. 'The women cannot dance. My wife … very disappointed.' He picked at something stuck to his beloved radio, his face assuming a hunted look, as if, in a thousand ways, Mrs Siyaka might cause him to be very disappointed too. The mud began to seep through the walls and the Chief of Iapnamal, a very dark, very stooped, very jumpy individual, launched into a Lear-like rant, wading around in the rain and bellowing at the skies. I asked Siyaka what he was saying. 'He wants to know who did it,' Siyaka explained. 'Who has made it rain.'

'Why are there no *pphwt* yams in England?' my neighbour mused, determined the conversation should not meander from its moorings, and equally unconcerned that no one else was joining in. 'What do you eat?'

Siyaka said it was like the Flood in the Bible. They had their own story about that, he explained. It concerned another of mountain god Kalbaben's sons, a being called Nasabl. Kalbaben had charged him with protecting Tanna from the rains, so Nasabl had rolled up the island like a leaf, so that it bobbed around upon the stormy waters, but did not sink. Afterwards, when the land was dry, he unrolled the leaf and Kalbaben said he had done well.

'Nasabl had a white skin,' Siyaka observed. 'Like you.'

'That's not Nasabl,' said my other neighbour. 'That's Mwatiktik. He lives on the mountain as well, and he's the god of the gardens and all the yams. He's not Kalbaben's son, he's his brother.'

'Brother-in-law,' Siyaka countered.

'You don't know anything, Siyaka!'

It was a very male conversation – no different to a pair of Englishmen clashing over the Arsenal line-up. But if anyone's opinion should be trusted on the matter of this pale-faced yam god, I thought, then it was the man who'd spoken about nothing but yams for the past two hours. It was useful, too.

Tanna was a unique place, not least for its geography: the easternmost point of Melanesia. Just forty nautical miles away, on neighbouring Futuna, the people were Polynesian, with lighter complexions and different myths and customs. From there across the thousand leagues of the Pacific ocean, as far as Hawaii, they told tales of a Polynesian hero named Maui-tiki-tiki-tao-a-taranga, and it wasn't hard to imagine this light-skinned figure creeping into Tannese tales as Mwatiktik. Nor to imagine another light-skinned hero called Philip being slotted in, in later years. I sat up, my spirits reviving slightly.

'And did either of these spirits sail away, over the sea?' I asked.

'Yes,' declared the yam fan. 'Mwatiktik came from another island. He sailed here from Futuna... But the yams there are...' He almost gagged at the thought of these inferior tubers.

'But did he sail anywhere else?' I prompted. 'You know, to...'

Siyaka held up a finger to make me quiet. It was clear he couldn't permit any discussions without some sort of verbal chitty from Nako, the increasingly Stalinist Minister of Information. I hoped I'd remember what I just learnt, because I was too weak to write it down.

I awoke around midnight and staggered into the roaring, pouring world outside to empty myself into the trench. On my return I nibbled at a piece of yam. Stomach-based skirmishes turned into total war. Four further trips to the little screened-off slit trench became necessary, the meteorological outrage mirroring the battles inside the one man braving it. With each foray I became weaker, less able to negotiate the swirling mists and spiteful mud.

And then, in the morning, I awoke to a vista of good things. Sunlight streamed through the walls of the shelter, the sodden earth had baked firm and Siyaka brought me warm bananas on a tin plate. Shaken but happy, I left the cursed village as part of a laughing, smiling gang and we all slid down to the cold, crystal torrent of the waterfall.

And then I really awoke. It was ten in the morning and the rain was still roaring down. My guts continued to roil, I was stiff with mud and shit. Nako, too vizier-like now to speak directly to me, relayed a message through Siyaka. It was likely the rain would last all day. We would have to stay here. I sensed Nako rather relished the idea, if only because he knew I hated it.

I received the news numbly, propped against the wooden slats of the shelter walls, too sick to care. I couldn't find my glasses. I squinted around the crowded space in bitter amazement. Now, the people of Tanna appalled me. Squatting blithely in the ash and mud, choking up the place with their smoky fires, utterly unconcerned at the fiasco outside. People spat on the very floor where they slept and sat, and they fried up bits of nastiness in blackened pans. This was bloody normal to them, I thought. They were happy. And I would perish here in this cage of filth, on top of a mountain of mud.

I couldn't have asked for a sharper clash between the Pacific I'd dreamed of, with its white sand and palm trees, and the reality. The Pacific was not paradise – and that surely had some part to play in the amount of utopia-promising cults I'd seen on Tanna. In a few, select places Australian honeymooners could purchase a fortnight of blue seas and smiling islanders slinging garlands as they strummed their guitars. But outside the confines of Pacific Paradise™, people had little. When they got sick – as a result of the lack of clean water – it was hard to get help because of the crappy roads. Governments sometimes diverted money away from the rural areas into impressive public works for their capitals, or even into their own pockets. Political debate, in some places, was still being thrashed out with guns and sticks. Traditional life was rich, with its ceremonies and its bags of free time, but it could also be tough.

And so I wondered, as I squatted in that slippery field of mud and shit, if that might be why nobody before me, save for the odd anthropologist, had bothered to investigate what Philippism really was. It was acceptable to print reports, by people who hadn't spent more than twenty-four hours on Tanna, stating little more than 'Oo-er blimey, look at these berks,' because we couldn't take the Pacific seriously in the first place.

The very name, Pacific, to people who hadn't been there, evoked peace and tranquillity. These happy islanders, with their woolly hair and their vivid shirts, were on permanent vacation. They venerated pigs, as well, beasts synonymous in our language – pigging out, pigsty, pig ignorant – with greed, slovenliness and stupidity. Then there was that language we used to communicate with them. Bislama, named after the French word for a sea-slug, and full of simpleton contortions. They couldn't be serious, could they?

And there were those so-called cargo cults. I'd read a hefty list by Lamont Lindstrom, a long-time Tanna expert, of all the times Western commentators exaggerated the cargo and ignored the aims of the cult.

Vending machines and fridges popped up with suspicious regularity in the newspaper accounts of what the cultists longed for, even though your average Melanesian tribesman would never even have heard of those things. We even brought our contempt home, using the term 'cargo cult' to denigrate anything that seemed irrational, ill thought out, or based on unrealistic expectations, from town planning to computer programming. It was as if our own obsession with stuff, combined with a basic contempt for dark-skinned people, had blinded us to what these Pacific movements really wanted: equality with the Europeans, clout, status, organisation, self-determining power. And I hadn't, as yet, encountered a single person on Tanna who was longing for a fridge, or who didn't know that money was the only means of getting one.

I needed to note some of this down. And I had eight postcards left, protected from the Tanna ash in a ziplock bag, but without my glasses I couldn't manage the tiny lettering that was necessary because of lack of space. I wouldn't be able to make any more notes at all. In desperation I started to pat the pulpy floor around my sleeping mat. Siyaka turned from the gang he'd been chatting with and asked me what was the matter. Within an instant, every man there was trawling the floor with his fingertips, like police after a murder. I felt ashamed. How could I be so cruel to them in my thoughts, these decent, gentle, generous people? They didn't like being trapped here any more than me. They were just being grown-up about it.

In a frenzy of efficiency Siyaka probed the thatched roof with his hands, causing a chunk of it to dislodge and anointing those below with a mixture of rainwater, bat droppings and straw. Apart from this, the search yielded nothing. I resigned myself to being partially sighted and noteless for the remainder of my time on Tanna. Maybe I'd lost my glasses on one of my slithering, shivering trips to that latrine trench. One day archaeologists would dig out a shit-encrusted pair of SpecSavers glasses and publish man-high theses about the incredible extent of Tannese exchange routes.

But a certain symmetry did not escape me. I'd ruffled feathers when I announced my intention to present a pair of spectacles to Chief Kowiya. The next day my own went missing. Nako had already proved his willingness to confiscate items from me…

'Yumi stap long calabus!' quipped Siyaka, shaking the sparse walls of the shelter. We're in jail. And it was exactly what I'd been thinking. I felt like a prisoner of war, a lone Brit on some remote island, penned into a wooden compound to perish of dysentery and defeat.

'He will be all right. He just needs a yam,' opined the Man City supporter, 'and probably some kava.'

At that moment I glimpsed a familiar pair of bright-red, baggy trousers waddling past the shelter. They could only have belonged to Daniel, the boy from

Imabel who'd been so helpful the day before. However rotten I felt, I had to talk to him some more. I staggered outside.

That flicker of red on the edge of my vision was all I had to go on in my spec-less state, so I followed it, skidding hopelessly in the mist and mud. Soon I had lost all sense of where the lad had gone, and was merely trying to put one foot in front of the other without losing my shoes. Like the three witches on the blasted heath, a group of ragged men in a makeshift booth hailed me.

'What are you doing?' asked the oldest, a grizzled figure in a T-shirt that said 'I ♥ Golf'.

'Looking for a man called Daniel,' I explained. 'He just went past here.'

'Nobody's come past here,' said the golf fan. 'Come and talk to us.'

I glanced around the field, seeing nothing now but monochrome mud and mist. The thought of going deeper into this seemed pretty disagreeable, so I went and sat with the cheerfully sodden triumvirate under their orange plastic sheeting, enjoying the warmth of their bodies. We talked, and the usual formalities concerning yams, kava and their geographical distribution around the globe were confused somewhat by the assumption that I was from New Zealand. Upon my making it clear where I did, in fact, come from, the old man became excited and said that he wanted to build a road with me.

'But you wouldn't want to build a road with me if I was from New Zealand?'

'We already have many roads with them.'

It was time to resolve this road issue for good. 'But New Zealand is a long way over the sea. How can you have a road to there?'

The old man frowned, and made some markings in the mud with the point of his knife. His afro was wider than it was high, and there was a reddish glow to his cheeks and nose. He looked like someone in a Dickens adaptation – a seedy clerk, perhaps, with a gin bottle under his desk, but of a morally sound disposition. He showed me his markings.

'You marry a girl from Tanna, you see, and then you take her to England. And when you have a daughter – that's this line here – you send her back, to marry a man from Tanna.' He replicated the pattern underneath. 'Then they have a daughter, see…'

'And they send her to England to marry a man there?'

He punched me, quite painfully, in the arm. 'Yes, yes! Swappem. That's a road.'

Another conceptual coconut dropped into the nakamal of knowledge. A road could be a relationship, an alliance of exchange, as well as something cut through the bush. I began to see why Chief Jack had been so emphatic about the roads of Tanna when we'd had our first proper chat, why he'd seemed so disappointed that I hadn't understood. Why Kirk Huffman had been described as a 'gate'. Why those men had been so miffed when I'd said I wouldn't build a road with them. Most importantly, why Yaohnanen had sent gifts and offered girls to Prince Philip, because they wanted a road with him – flinging out a sort of lasso that was at once symbolic and political, spiritual and economic. Was this more of the Tannese drive to reunite things split apart, to restore the rift in creation?

'So what happens when you've built roads everywhere?' I asked. 'When you've opened a road between every village on Tanna and from every village on Tanna to every place in the rest of the world?'

'Oh dear, Matthew!' boomed a voice to the left of me. 'Why hasn't Nako explained these things?'

I looked with weary resignation at Lomakom, arrayed in a T-shirt and shorts of dazzling cleanliness, and snugly installed under a gaily striped umbrella at the mouth of our little kiosk. Nobody, I thought, could stay so spotless by honest means alone.

'Where is your friend? I thought he had you on a piece of rope?'

I shrugged, too tired to mind the obvious mockery. 'Why are you and Nako so angry with each other?'

'Oh, I like Nako,' Lomakom said. 'But he has been insulting me every day.'

'Every day?'

'Every day some village is hearing all about Prince Philip and his new school and all the wonderful things that are going to happen… But not my village.'

'I've only been to one village so far. Two, if you count this one. And Philip hasn't got anything to do with the new school. I just gave some money so they could build it. I haven't done anything except read out some stories, that came from here, from Tanna.'

'I know exactly what you've been doing,' Lomakom said, with the dark, meaningful tone of a man trying to sell you some locally produced porn in a pub.

'I don't know what you mean, but if you're angry about not having heard the stories, then I'll read them for you.'

Lomakom tapped his front tooth with a fingernail, winked at one of the seated men and then flashed me a sub-zero smile. 'All right,' he said, squatting down in the circle. 'Tell me one of these famous stories from Philip.'

'OK,' I said, taking a deep breath. I didn't bother to correct him about the stories being from Tanna, not from Prince Philip. I had a different strategy in mind. 'When Kwin Lisbet was a young girl, she went on a boat with her father, who was the King of England. And they went to a special school, where the boys were learning to be sailors. And they looked around the school, and then they sailed away on their big boat. And the young boys went out after them, in their little boats, to wave goodbye.'

I glanced around the shelter. Everyone was listening, none more intently than Lomakom. 'Most of them turned back to the shore, but one little boat kept following them. And the King said, "Who is that foolish boy in that little boat? He will get himself drowned." And the King waved at him, angrily, to send him away. But just before he turned the boat back, the boy in the boat stood up and gave a salute. And Kwin Lisbet saw him – he was a young, tall blond man, very handsome and she fell in love with him. That man was Prince Philip.'

'Hmm,' said Lomakom. He spat delicately on the ground and then gazed around the group. 'This is what they're talking about in Yaohnanen?'

I said nothing. Out of respect for Chief Jack, if no one else, I hadn't given Lomakom and his cronies a Philip myth – not a Tannese one, anyway. It was a story from the richly embellished account of Marion Crawford, or 'Crawfie', Queen Elizabeth's later discredited nanny.

'This story just proves what idiots they are,' Lomakom sneered. 'If he's a boy at school in England, then he's English, so how can he be from Tanna?'

'He's not English.'

'Where is he from?' Lomakom countered, chuckling. 'America, like John Frum?'

'His uncle was the King of Greece, but the family came from Denmark. You know Denmark?'

'I've seen it on maps,' Lomakom replied loftily. 'So why does a chief of Denmark end up in Greece?'

'Because there was no King in Greece.'

'Why not?'

I wasn't sure it was the right place to start talking about the Ottoman Empire, or Lord Byron, or the various ancestors of Philip who'd been assassinated and poisoned by monkey bites. I stumbled through it, though, and ended up telling them how Philip's uncle, King Constantine, had been deposed in 1922.

'Philip was very small then, and they didn't have time to bring his bed, so he left Greece in a little wooden box, the kind we ship oranges in. And they went to France, and he was so poor that when he was at school and it was raining like today, he had to stay in the schoolhouse until it stopped, because he didn't have a coat.'

Softer elements of the crowd shook their heads, their hearts pricked with sympathy for the poor coat-less boy and his orange-crate bed. I sat back in the mud, drained from the effort of speaking, awaiting Lomakom's response.

'Rubbish stories,' he pronounced finally. He got to his feet and bent down to me. He smelt, disconcertingly, of fabric conditioner. 'You think we all believe in magic, and children's stories, and if you tell us a lot of lies, we'll just start to follow you. Ha!' And he stalked off, untroubled by the mud, seeming to hover a few millimetres above it.

It was true what I'd told him, though, every last detail. But I began to wonder if Philip's extraordinary life story could have contributed to his status, here and at home. Perhaps his pan-European ancestry and some odd snippets of his rags-to-riches tale had trickled back to the faith makers of Yaohnanen, making him, for reasons I had yet to understand, the perfect object for their devotions.

And maybe, too, that was why he'd failed to find a place in British hearts. It is human to fear the ambiguous, the thing that is neither this nor that. Philip's aunt, Princess Marie Bonaparte, had been a direct descendant of Napoleon, as well as an early member of the weird Austrian cult called psychoanalysis. His sister Sophia married high-ranking Nazi Prince Christoph of Hesse. At a regimental dinner commemorating the Battle of Balaclava, Philip had once admitted, with a sheepish grin, that his relatives had been fighting on the other side. 'Phil the Greek' is French, German, Russian and Danish. By his mere presence he reminds us that the Queen of England, his third cousin, is not particularly English, and nor, for that matter, are we.

Wherever, in anthropology, you find such ambiguity, you find notions of taboo and danger. Whether it's multi-national monarchs, boys on the brink of circumcision, or brides on the eve of their weddings, you find an idea that such people are dangerous, bringers of bad luck or disease. Prince Philip – like Victoria's husband, Prince Albert – has an additional burden to bear. To be the husband of a queen, but not a king, is an anomaly that sets our most primal alarm bells a-ringing. Albert faced a rough time for his German fashions and his eccentric hobbies. And the same was true for Philip – long before he'd begun to offend people with his unfashionable sense of humour.

As early as 1942, newspaper readers learned he'd been injured, not honourably, but staggering shit-faced around the streets of Chelsea in the blackout. When Charles was born, the royal couple demanded privacy, giving rise to press rumours that the boy was malformed, unspoken charges of bad blood and inbreeding lying just between the lines. Later Philip was linked, without a shred of evidence, to actress Merle Oberon, heiress Susan Barrantes, a string of nameless nymph-like creatures called 'showgirls', and finally made central villain of a Bond plot involving the bumping off of his own daughter-in-law, Princess Diana. There is no act of which the mythic Philip has not been considered capable, because he is *homo liminus*, not possessing one particular passport, nor a kingly crown, untouchable and thoroughly taboo.

And the murky waters of our own Philip cult had flowed, inevitably, into the way we viewed the one in the Pacific. In a place we rarely took seriously anyway, people worshipped a man whom we, for our own anthropological reasons, reviled.

At this point someone came pushing through the sodden crowd, a steely gleam in his eyes. I made it, shakily, to my feet, expecting another tussle with Nako. But he simply said, very slowly, fighting the kava for every syllable, that some men wanted to meet me, sorcerers, in a hut over the way. So I went with him across that god-ravaged landscape, forced, in my shame, to hold onto his shoulder.

In a light, comfortable, square-built hut, five men were waiting on brightly coloured mats. I could only make out the two closest to me in detail. One was gaunt and wore a balaclava. Another was very stout – he had a patrician's beard and a Palestinian keffiyeh around his neck, giving him the look of an area manager for the Mujahidin. Their features were sharp, their eyes bright, their movements quick. I felt I was in the company of clever men, leaders, thinkers. And indeed this was the name by which sorcerers were known in Bislama – kleva.

The klevas greeted me gravely with a bowl of kava. I thought it might at least numb my stomach, so I swallowed it down, followed by a handful of peanuts. Neither helped much.

The senior Mujahid kicked things off by asking me my father's name, and then Prince Philip's father's name. 'Anthony,' I repeated, rather disappointed to be subjected to another bout of the name game. 'Andrea.'

'They are the same name,' he concluded, learnedly.

'No, they are not,' I replied. 'An-tow-nee,' I spelled out. 'An-dray-aa.'

'Same name.'

'No, not same name.'

'So you live in the same village as Prince Philip,' the Mujahid said, with the deliberate, theatrical air of a learned QC. 'But you say you are not of his line?'

'It's a very big village.'

'Do you want us to tell you the truth?'

'Yes please.'

'Do you agree, that if we tell you the truth, you will tell us the truth?'

'Yes.'

'Are you of the line of Prince Philip?'

I was becoming irritated now, particularly as I'd noticed how clean and dry the klevas all were, having passed the accursed night in the comforts of their own little clubhouse. Perhaps Lomakom had been with them, I thought. There certainly seemed to be something supernatural about the way he kept popping up.

'It is only he says that because you are coming from the same village as the Prince Philip,' Nako slurred, after a brief exchange in Nauvhal. 'They say he is the chief of that village, so it should be that all of the people in it are of his line. I also did explain to them that it is not your way on your island belonging to you.' He belched sonorously. 'And they did understand now.'

'I see,' I said, relieved. 'Thank you. No … sorry, not the same line.'

'Well, you look like him,' replied the Mujahid rather sulkily.

Talk moved on to the myths, and Nako granted me permission to read them. I thought it was worth a try. I was in the company of middle-aged men, and that meant, to my thinking, a high probability of them having had been old enough to remember the cult's beginnings.

'Philip continues the work Jake Raites and John Frum did not complete,' I recited, reading more from my collection. 'It is through his word that they built the hospital on Tanna. With his magic, he made Kwin Lisbet dream about a white building, night after night, until she spent all her waking hours thinking of it too. Then Philip suggested they hold a competition, and ask all the students of the world to draw the building that Lisbet saw in her dreams. Drawing after drawing came to the Palace where they lived, but Lisbet could not see the building. Then one day, it came – a boy from Tanna drew it. To thank him, Lisbet sent money to build the building on Tanna, and it became the hospital.'

'We know this story,' said the Mujahid, nodding.

'You do?' This was good news.

'I can even tell you who the boy was, the boy who drew the building.'

'Will you tell me?'

'Yes. The boy was invited onto the boat when Kwin Lisbet came. And then he became a man. And that man is sitting HERE.'

With a conjuror's flourish he gestured to the shuffling, grinning, hawk-like presence in the balaclava. He did not, it must be noted, resemble someone who would be allowed near a Royal Yacht.

'This man is Joe Keitu,' thundered the Mujahid, 'and he made the drawing and he went on board the boat. By the spirit. Do you understand? By the spirit.'

'Right.'

'He is a famous kleva of Tanna, he can count his family back twelve generations and he has the power to travel everywhere by the spirit. This man' – here Joe Keitu's official spokesperson waved his hand towards the others in the hut – 'and this man, and this man, we are all the followers of Joe Keitu. Prince Philip is also a follower of Joe Keitu. Prince Philip has sent him a letter.'

I leant forward in spite of my quivering stomach. 'What did it say?'

The Mujahid glanced at Joe Keitu, who gave a mercurial waggle of his helmeted head. Another of the men – a very small gent in wellington boots – trotted to the side of the hut and fetched a wide, flat piece of wood, many times larger than himself. He returned, grunting slightly, with the wood, to which a letter bearing the Buckingham Palace crest had been glued. I blinked in amazement.

'Prince Philip sent a letter congratulating him,' the Mujahid said proudly. 'For his work in manufacturing Western medicines. Including paracetamol.'

The letter wasn't from Prince Philip at all. It was from Buckingham Palace, though. It had been written by Brigadier Sir Miles Hunt-Davis a year ago, thanking a photographer in New Caledonia for sending Prince Philip some pictures of village life.

'How did you get this?'

'By the spirit,' replied the Mujahid briskly. 'Now tell me. Is it true that all white men hate Prince Philip?'

'Not so much hate,' I said, tearing my eyes away from the extraordinary trophy. 'And it's not all white people. Just in Britain, really. A man in Milwaukee sent him a duffel coat once. As a wedding present.' Everybody stared at me, and reasonably enough, I supposed, if they didn't know what a duffel coat or a wedding present or Milwaukee was. 'Milwaukee's in America,' I added weakly.

Joe Keitu cleared his throat, and then licked his lips. 'It was a black man who sent him that coat,' he murmured.

'I suppose it could have been, yes.' I smiled encouragingly at the renowned sorcerer, but he offered nothing else for the duration of our meeting.

Presently the Mujahid clapped his hands and, to my astonishment, a long line of people, all ages, shapes, genders and T-shirts, filed in, shook my hand and walked out again. The procedure took about fifteen minutes, and by the end of it I felt dazed.

'Has this all been helpful?' enquired the Mujahid politely.

'Erm…' The meeting had told me nothing about the myths, or those wider questions of worship, but it proved, beyond doubt, that the veneration of Philip, in one form or another, was to be found all over the island. It was alive, whatever lies Lomakom poured in my ear. 'Yes,' I said, at length. 'Very much. Thank you.'

'So please now help us. Please write your name for us.'

I rummaged through my shoulder bag, remembering as I did so, a little tale about Prince Philip being asked to sign the guest book at a London club before his advantageous marriage bumped him into the limelight. 'Philip,' he'd written, simply, and was hoyed back by the clerk to add a surname. 'Of Greece,' he'd added drily.

'Why do you smile?' asked the Mujahid.

'No reason.' I couldn't spare anything from my diminishing selection of Sydney postcards, so settled for the final leaf of an ancient chequebook that had been lying in the gritty netherworld of my bag for at least two years. I tore it out, scribbled my name, and handed it over. The klevas clustered around it.

'Thanks. You can go now,' said the Mujahid, barely glancing up from the slip of paper in his hands.

So I left them in their hut and hacked my way across the boggy field towards the shelter. Halfway there, I felt a strange sensation in the sleeve of my left arm. I poked a finger through the slit next to the cuff and something shot out to land in the sludge at my feet. It was my spectacles.

Back in the shelter, I showed Siyaka, who, in his enthusiasm to tell others of the miraculous reappearance of my eyewear, snapped the right arm clean off them. Klevas found lost objects all the time, he enthused, trying dangerously to reattach the ear-piece with mud-encrusted fingers, that was their main job. Sometimes the police even got them in for murder investigations.

If this were true, I thought, quietly removing my glasses from further harm, then no one would have been so surprised by what happened to me. But they were. Even so, I couldn't explain it. I'd gone through every inch of my own clothing when I was looking for them. My shirt was loose, not tucked into my trousers, and I'd moved around pretty vigorously in my attempts to find Daniel and get across the muddy fields. I'd shaken hands with a great long line of people, of course, but that had been with my right hand.

'Your belly is better?' Siyaka asked.

'Yes. Yes it is,' I replied distractedly. Somehow, at some point in that meeting with the sorcerers, the storm in my stomach had given way to calm. The rains had stopped too, and the first hesitant fingers of sunlight were curling their way through the clouds.

'We'll go back to our village,' Siyaka said, shouldering his ancient kitbag, and in the process giving a bloody nose to a frail old Chief who'd had the poor judgement to be standing close by. When this had been mopped up and restorative shells of kava administered all round, even to people who'd been a considerably long way away at the time of the incident, we were finally ready to leave.

'I'd like to just look for someone before we go,' I told Siyaka, scanning the steaming horizon with my newly restored sight. 'Boy called Daniel, from Imabel.'

'Don't know him.'

'You know – the guy I was talking to last night. When Nako got angry. Red trousers. Big hair.'

Siyaka shook his head. But before I could pursue the point, a great agitated gang of men surged towards us, the Mujahid at its head and moving, it had to be said, very nimbly for a fat man.

'I will ask you one more time,' boomed the big man, 'to tell us the truth. Are you of the line of Prince Philip?'

'No.'

'But this is money, isn't it?' With a flourish the Mujahid produced the old cheque I'd given them.

'A kind of money,' I conceded. 'A letter you write instead of money.'

The Mujahid thrust it in my face and ran his finger along the address line of my bank. And I groaned inwardly. I should have been more careful, bearing in mind the name of the busy Belgravia street where my branch was located.

'If you are not of Prince Philip's line,' thundered my interrogator, 'then why do you have the letter-you-write-instead-of-money of the road of Buckingham Palace in your bag?'

'It's just because Buckingham Palace Road is...'

'IT'S BECAUSE PHILIP SENT YOU HERE WITH A MESSAGE FOR US!'

'I don't have a message for you.'

'Then you have a message for John Frum.'

Later in the day, after we'd escaped the klevas and their accusations, I lay weakly on a rock by the river and thumbed through some notes on the John Frum movement, trying to understand if, or how, it fitted in with Philippism. I realised I wasn't the only white man to have been frustrated by Tannese cultism.

In November 1940 James Nichol, the British government's District Agent on Tanna, received a complaint from members of the Seventh Day Adventist Church. They said villagers in the south-western settlement of Green Point had been holding mass gatherings, and that their goats had been killed to feed them. The crowds were flocking to hear a shadowy figure called John Frum. He spoke in a high-pitched voice, and astonished his audiences by exposing people who had been slacking off communal work tasks. Nichol sent three deputies to investigate. To his fury, they all came back as ardent believers in John Frum. He went to Green Point himself, and arrested the two men who first claimed to have met John – Messrs Kohu and Karaua – keeping them at the police station until the gathering dispersed. Things went quiet.

Six months later Nichol took a holiday. And in the absence of the government man the Tannese began a rush on the shops. People were buying up goods in a frenzy, spending more than £1000 in one month, despite a slump in copra prices. Cattle and pigs were slaughtered to feed the crowds at all-night dances being held each night in a different village. On 11 May not one soul attended the Presbyterian service at the church in Lenakel.

Tanna wasn't the first place where this has happened. In the 1880s, in Fiji, the British authorities had taken stern measures against a prophet called Navosavakadua, who had received visions of the chucking out of the whites and the arrival of a ship, staffed by the ancestors, bearing a giant cargo of calico and tinned fish. Throughout New Guinea there'd been so many similar cultic flurries that a local newspaper had started running a column called 'How You Get It', trying to convince the natives that the Europeans' coveted knives and canned food and engines were made in far-away factories, not whistled up by magic.

On Tanna, John Frum's message began to change, speaking of an end-of-days scenario, and a shucking off of white rule. Everyone must leave the mission, stop going to church, stop sending their kids to school, and return to kastom. The whites would leave, people said, and the Tannese would have their houses. One follower had this to say to a baffled trader: 'Bambae mane belong me i kam, be fes belong yufala King, tek em e go bak'. My money will come. This stuff with your King's face on it, take it back.

Resident Europeans began to fear an uprising. Nichol requested back-up troops from Port Vila and went to Green Point, looking for this upstart Frum. Fingers pointed to an old man called Manehivi, noted in his village for the possession of a white, brass-buttoned naval jacket. After twenty-four hours with Nichol, this elderly gentleman confessed to impersonating John Frum. He was tied to a coconut tree for a day and then he and Karaua were sent to jail in Port Vila. It later emerged that he was a stool pigeon, who knew nothing about the cult.

Meanwhile the local worthies begged forgiveness and offered £100 to pay for the extra police. Nichol accepted this and had his men burn down the temporary house built for John Frum. It was forbidden to mention Frum's name.

But mentioned he was. In January 1942 Nichol intercepted letters from Port Vila to a Green Point man. The letters came from Joe Nalpin, a Tanna man now part of the police in Port Vila. Joe had written to his father that the son of John Frum would be sent by aeroplane to search for 'the King'. The letter also said John Frum was the 'broom' who would sweep away the whites.

A Scots engineer outwitted by a spirit. It was all too much. As Nichol dealt with this fresh outrage, Tanna men threatened a Chinese trader. They forced him to sell his shop, telling him that soon he and other foreigners would be leaving. A fresh orgy of spending had begun in the stores. Nichol took drastic action. By the end of the year some twenty-nine Green Point men had been jailed in Port Vila without trial. Two died while in custody. Twelve were eventually released in April 1949.

Nichol's own view of the causes of the disturbances was oddly insightful. The mission had outlawed the only sources of fun: kava and dancing, and people wanted them back. People also resented the Sabbath because it prevented them from working in their gardens. Nichol further suggested that the slump in copra prices had caused insecurity, particularly as locals, with no insight into the global economy, just thought the traders were being mean when they lowered their prices.

Anthropologists, understandably, love the John Frum cult as much as photographers do. It happens on a well-appointed, friendly island, where there are minimal risks of being stung or shot. Its followers display a fascinating mix of American, military and kastom-related symbolism, and they communicate in a language not terribly hard to master. So anthro-friendly is the Frum phenomenon that, nearly seventy years later, people are still publishing theses on the subject. And none of them can agree on its causes.

The French anthropologist Jean Guiart, who interviewed many of its early leaders in the post-war period, was told the movement had originally been devised only to put Christianity to the test. If it really 'worked', it would be able to withstand the shock of rebellion. Other people have pointed out that the arrival of Seventh Day Adventists and Catholics in the 1930s had already weakened the Presbyterians' grip. As it became possible to opt into a rival Christian team without dire consequences, others saw it was possible to opt out altogether, and return to the earthy embrace of kastom. The rout was extensive: by 1942 there were only seven Presbyterians left in Lenakel, the main town. The mission at White Sands had ninety-one followers, as opposed to some nine hundred BJF (Before John Frum).

We're not certain about the root of the name John Frum. Joe Nalpin's letter said Frum was the 'broom' to sweep away the whites – and in Vanuatu today some newspapers routinely call it the 'John Brum/Broom' cult. Others suggest it may have been a friendly visitor, explaining himself as 'John from...' somewhere. Anthropologist Lamont Lindstrom points to the similarity between 'Frum' and the local word 'urumun', meaning a spirit medium.

We will never unpick the truth, because there isn't one, or not just one. Different people will always join a cult for different reasons. But John Frum was here to stay, and as the Japanese bombed Pearl Harbour in December 1941, prompting the USA to enter World War Two, the Tannese were ready to take stock of yet another cargo of puzzling foreigners.

I, for my part, had a feeling of entering some Promised Land as I limped with Siyaka and the hissing radio set across the familiar little brook marking the edge of Yaohnanen land. Soon we were by the log which led to my hut. And the bees buzzed and the afternoon sun splashed the whole scene with gold, and a butterfly settled on the snow-white curls of the Chief, who'd padded out to greet me.

'Village belong yumi,' said Siyaka.

Yumi. I grinned at him and the Chief. A simple pronoun that massaged my soul.

Where plurals were concerned, Bislama could become extremely complicated. It discriminated, depending on the number of people being referred to, and whether the person being spoken to was included or not. 'Belong mifala' was 'ours-but-not-yours', but 'belong yumi' meant the chummy, inclusive, 'mine-

and-yours'. A minuscule shift in grammar, but that 'yumi' was like a slap on the back.

And I sat on my orange plastic chair in the sunlight, rejoicing at the way its legs sank into the soft soil. Inside the hut were clean clothes, a radio that worked, a sleeping bag, soap. Everything there, from the reed roof to Nako's shredded underpants seemed wreathed in luminous, loving light, dry and warm and good, as if the whole scene and all its constituent parts were smiling at me.

'But you were not glad at the ceremony,' Chief Jack said delicately.

'I wasn't very well,' I admitted, removing my crusted socks.

'That is because our ancestors are looking after you here. All around,' the Chief said, gesturing around, as if pointing to some recent plastering work he'd done. 'But they couldn't look after you in Iapnamal... It is a very wicked place.'

Siyaka nodded. 'The Chief of Iapnamal got Joe Keitu to visit the spirit world and bring him back lots of money. That's why it rained and spoiled the ceremony.'

'Some people said maybe you were the one making it rain.'

I looked at them in alarm. 'Me?'

'Don't worry,' Siyaka said. 'I told them. White men have cameras. They don't have any magic.'

It had been very different, I thought, as I settled

down for bed that night, at the height of cargo-cult fever in the early twentieth century. It had all started with a basic observation. Black men worked to grow their food and make the few goods they owned. White men appeared to do nothing; they just sat at desks, made marks on pieces of paper and then, months later, cargo ships appeared, laden with impressive, manu-factured stuff. Pacific islanders concluded that magic had to be involved, some magic the Europeans were refusing to share with the blacks. It was suggested that they'd torn some pages out of the Bible when they brought it to the islands – the pages explaining how to get hold of all the coveted goods. That the whites had given the blacks a half-truth, or, as one disgruntled local summed up his experience of mission Christian-ity: *sing-sing nomo.* Just a load of singing. In an effort to crack the secret, islanders employed a variety of tac-tics: dressing like Europeans, or going naked, putting flowers in vases, or dancing all day, eating at tables, or consuming all their precious pigs. Faulty premises, but rational strategies. And that, increasingly, was how I thought of Philippism: not just a weird idea, but a tactic, a means of achieving something, that might or might not have succeeded.

My thoughts were interrupted as Nako came crash-ing into the hut. We hadn't spoken, or even been in one another's company since the breakfast conference with Joe Keitu and his strange committee. Lord knows where he'd been. But now, it seemed, Nako wanted to speak.

'I am sorry we live in rubbish way,' he announced formally as he flopped onto the earthen floor.

I sat up in my sleeping bag. 'What?'

'I say sorry to you *pphwt* that we live in rubbish fashion.'

I swung my legs over the sleeping platform, alarmed. I could just about make out his shape by the embers of the fire – hunched in one of the stiff, Chinese-made blankets that offered approximately the same comfort as a square of Axminster. 'Nako – why do you say that?'

'Because you are not glad. You do not eat our island food. To you it is not good our way. You see how we live. We sleep just on the ground like this. We have not many clothes. Lap-lap, yam, all the time.' He cleared his throat noisily. 'I am sorry for our way. *Pphwt.*'

I was appalled. I sensed in Nako's words shame at his own way of life, a shame I'd unwittingly made him feel, just through being ill and confused. Perhaps that was what lay behind his moods and his anger. I felt ashamed I had ever believed Lomakom, ever suspected Nako of pursuing a private agenda. If he had the courage to address me in this way, he was a man of honour.

An apology tumbled out of me. I did not think he lived in rubbish way, I insisted. I had just been unwell. I was very pleased to be here, to learn about his life. I wanted to stay. I hoped he believed me.

'OK,' he said. '*Pphwt.* But I am sorry.'

'No. I am sorry.'

'It is finished,' Nako said. I lay back down on the log platform, staring up into the conical roof. Seconds later a delicate cough broke the silence. 'Er … that perfume…'

'The aftershave?' I sat up again. 'Do you want it now?'

'No. But you will give it into my hands when you fly away?'

'Yes. I promised.'

There was silence. 'But watch yourself, Nako,' I added. 'You put that aftershave on your face, and it's like masing. You know, it's like that magic potion Siyaka was telling me about – the one that makes girls fall in love with you. You will have to carry a big stick, so you can beat the women away.'

'Magic potion – ha!'

Silence. Then a solitary, sizzling *pphwt*, as Nako aimed spit onto the embers of the fire. I kicked myself under the blankets. At a sensitive point in our relations I had to go mucking it up with a silly comment. No wonder everyone thought I was related to Prince Philip.

'Good joking,' Nako pronounced suddenly. 'Good night.' And he gave a dry little chuckle. 'Masing … ha. Big stick. Yes, I will carry a big stick to Imabel tomorrow.'

'We're going to go to Imabel?'

'Yes, and my father says he will walk at the side of us and he will tell you everything. Everything,' he added portentously, 'that you do not know but you will. *Pphwt.*'

CHAPTER SIX

In Which the Venerable Old Chief of Yakel Receives His Gifts and Gives Back Little Except Attitude

'WHAT is the name of your Church, brother? Is it a very big Church? Is it the biggest Church in your country? Is it the…?'

'For the last time, I haven't got a Church!'

I didn't mean to sound so irritable. But this was becoming a pattern. In the mornings Nako would be mysteriously absent, and I would emerge from the hut, inappropriately clad, ill-prepared, sometimes even sporting the remains of an erection, to find a party of eager faces, whose owners sought something I could never deliver. This morning, feeling the dawn mists creeping up my boxer shorts, I'd stumbled over the hut's threshold to behold the beaming, bearded face of the Missionary from Iatanas, with a handful of earnest followers.

'I'm sorry,' I said, more gently. 'I'm interested in religions. All religions. But I don't go to a church because I'm not a Christian.'

The Missionary went into a huddle with his parishioners.

'They say you must be a man of Christ. Because those stories are Christian stories.'

I glanced at the tiny congregation – recognising upon their breasts the club colours of Aston Villa and Newcastle United, and even the face of New Jersey's soft-rock sensation Jon Bon Jovi, but not their owners. The women, certainly, could not have been present when I'd read out the Prince Philip myths, because they were banned from the nakamal – so how did they know about them?

'Wait a minute.'

I wormed my way into some clothes inside the hut, padded out and then, to escape further observation, went deep into the bush to relieve myself. A woman said something to the Missionary as I returned, damp with dew.

'She says she hopes that you made good water.'

'Thank you,' I said distractedly, pulling up the plastic chair. The woman said something else, and the Missionary flashed me a great yellow grin.

'She asks if your water is still green.'

'A little bit. Now, about these myths...'

'A man in her village had this green water.'

'Did he?'

'Yes. Before he died.'

'Can we just talk about the stories? Please?' The Missionary shrugged, a little regretfully, and allowed me to carry on. 'Those stories are kastom stories.'

'Yes, they are. When Prince Philip leaves Tanna on a white horse,' the Missionary replied, beaming so hard that his face seemed on the verge of cracking, 'that is in the Book of Revelation. Chapter six, verse two.' He took a deep breath and continued, 'I saw heaven standing open and before me a white horse, whose rider is called Faithful and True. With justice he judges and makes war.' As he recited, he swayed from side to side. Some of his parishioners now held up their hands, palms towards me. 'His eyes are like blazing fire, and on his head, many crowns. He has a name written on him that no one knows but him.'

'That's interesting, but...'

'Out of his mouth comes a sharp sword to strike down the nations.'

'That doesn't actually sound very like...'

'He treads the winepress of the fury of the wrath of God Almighty,' the Missionary concluded.

'None of that sounds like Prince Philip,' I pointed out, perhaps a little sharply. This outburst met with beady eyes, so I tried a more reasonable tone. 'In the myths, he's bringing peace and salvation. Curing sickness. Stopping wars. He doesn't go round striking down nations.'

'Perhaps, but the suit of gold and silver is from the Book of Daniel,' the Missionary continued, almost petulantly. 'The Dream of Nebuchadnezzar.' He took a deep breath again, but I held up a prohibitory hand.

'I'll look it up.'

And I intended to. Because even if Philippism was a kastom movement, it could well have incorporated Christian ideas. Most movements in the region drew from a common wellspring of notions about the End of Days, inspired by, if not faithful to, the details of the Bible. Men like Naiva and Tuk could have received some rudimentary education from the mission schools. And I was pretty certain that the stuff about the old men becoming young, and the disappearance of sickness and death, likewise had a Biblical origin.

The woman who had enquired about my morning micturition now addressed a very long speech to me in Nauvhal. In the Melanesian way, she indicated her deference by gazing straight upwards as she spoke, giving the impression that something very heavy was just about to land upon our heads.

'She says the old men used to talk about these things with a Frenchman who lived here,' the Missionary explained. 'His name was...' He paused to clarify something with the woman. 'John Gare.'

'Jean Guiart?'

'Yes. She says he had a book of pictures. And there

was a picture of Prince Philip. All bronze and silver, like Nebuchadnezzar's Dream.'

I looked directly at the woman and she hid her face in her hands.

'She is still afraid. Because she heard her grandfather talking about it in the nakamal when she was very young.

'I understand. Can I ask her … what was her grandfather's name?'

The Missionary gazed at me coolly. 'If you pray with us,' he said. 'She might tell you.'

Before I could reply, Mount Yasur, slumbering since the first morning of my stay on Tanna, gave a brief, dyspeptic belch. The soil quivered and the trees shook.

'I don't think the volcano wants me to pray,' I quipped. The Missionary's eyes widened. 'That was a joke,' I added quickly. Blank faces all around. 'Look,' I said. 'Tell me something. I don't recognise this lady. I don't recognise that gentleman there.' I pointed to a pained-looking character in a Christmas-tree jumper. 'So how do they know so much about my stories?'

'They heard them.'

'You mean they were there? When I read them out?'

'No, when…'

Angry words came from behind. Nako and Kal had emerged from the trees. Things were said, not happy things. The Missionary and his party scuttled away, with an almost pitying glance back at me.

'I was talking to them, Nako.'

'My father wants to see you,' Nako said. 'If you want to talk to that missionary again later, I will take you.'

'I thought we were going to Imabel.'

'After seeing my father.'

Somehow, not because of any psychic powers on my part, I knew this was bullshit. And I knew Chief Jack wouldn't be in the village when we walked to it. I knew exactly what was coming, and it involved two hours of sitting on a log, ignored, while Nako and his brother smoked and spat and discussed me.

Eventually the Chief did appear, without any sign of having summoned me or expected to see me. As I had him there, I asked if he remembered Jean Guiart's book, with the pictures of Prince Philip. I'd learnt about the man through royal picture books, and now, it seemed, with startling symmetry, the Tannese had been doing the same thing. A man of bronze and silver, Philip encrusted with medals, perhaps, striking a chord with men who'd also remembered Bible stories and older myths of some light-skinned god who'd gone away.

'John Gare,' the old Chief mused, lifting his nose into the air as if the memory could be smelt. 'Yes, I knew him. Big friend of kastom.'

A different type of white man, I thought, remembering what Kirk Huffman had told me, about how the anthropologist Guiart had set up home on the island and fought for justice for Frumists who'd been imprisoned and exiled. What a stark contrast he must have made, to all those rapacious traders and meddling missionaries and distant government men. I wondered how the Tannese had made sense of this sea-change in the spirit of their invaders.

'He showed us many things in his books. And when we saw a picture of Philip, we asked if he was Man England. And John Gare said, no, not Man England. So we asked if he was Man Franis. No, not Man Franis, John Gare said. Not Man Ostralia. Not Man New Zeelan. Not Man Amerika. So ... we understood what John Gare meant. If Philip is from none of these places, then there is only one other place he can come from.'

'Where?'

'Tanna!'

He gave a little clap. And as he did so, as if he'd conjured it into my mind, I could picture the scene. A French anthropologist, probably no great fan of British royalty, chuckling over the Queen of England's husband and his distinctly un-English ancestry. And his words, taken by the Tannese, given a dusting of mysticism and stewed almost out of recognition in a thousand fireside kava sessions. Untroubled by the circumstances whereby a Danish noble ended up as a Greek prince and then a Scottish thane, the Tannese anchored this man's origins in the only place that mattered to them.

'In the picture, he had a coat,' Chief Jack recalled, waving a trembling hand across his bare chest, 'gold here, silver there.'

'Just do that again.'

'Gold here,' he said, pointing to his right, 'and silver there,' as he moved his hand to the left.

Just as Tuk Noao had said on the BBC film – just like the story, where Queen Elizabeth stood on Philip's left side. Gold meant black, and right-handed and the colour of kastom, and white was the silver and the left. Did they glimpse in the form of Prince Philip some composite figure, uniting black and white, plugging up the chasm that caused rancour in the created world?

I was so delighted by what I felt to have been revealed, that I almost overlooked something important. This was Chief Jack, telling me important stuff about the origins of Philippism. Yet when I'd first arrived, he and everyone else had acted as if they'd never heard of the cult, almost as if I'd been bringing news of it to them. So what had changed? Had they just begun to trust me?

'Thank you for telling me this. I'm sorry I haven't managed to find anything out about the stories yet,' I said carefully – watching for his response.

'Keep asking,' the Chief said, patting my leg. 'When the road is difficult, you do not leave it and go into the bush, you stay with it. Don't forget now.' He mimed a microphone. 'When you go to a village, tell the stories and ask if they know them.' He wagged a finger at me. 'We must find out.'

Was it my imagination, or was there a slightly naughty air to the Chief's injunction – something quite different to the aggrieved way he'd first charged me to investigate the missing myths? I sensed he was having fun with me. And perhaps it didn't matter. I was finding things out all the time now, as if, to use a Tannese metaphor, some blockage had been lifted from the road of knowledge, and a shipment of good things was coming my way.

'Well, I'll read the stories again today,' I promised, glancing across at Nako, 'when we go to Imabel.'

Nako and Chief Jack shook their heads. 'Cannot to Imabel today,' Nako said, clearing his throat. 'Kowiya has spoken along the road. We must to give to his hand today the thing you have to give to him from Cook Gavman.'

'Give him the spectacles from Kirk Huffman?'

'For a long time the road was blocked,' Chief Jack reflected. 'Now, because of you, Kowiya sends a kava branch along it.' He spat, thoughtfully. 'It is a good thing. Too long fighting.'

'This is why my father was telling you about the book belonging John Gare,' Nako said gravely. 'Because you are a gate.'

'I'm a gate?'

'You opened the road,' Chief Jack confirmed. 'Kolassis!' he suddenly exclaimed, using the Bislama word for spectacles. 'Let me see them!' He gave a dry chuckle as I produced the reading glasses from their bubble-wrap and put them on. His old, pale eyes assumed an unsettling, marine quality, like some kraken on the floor of the sea. Even Nako smiled.

'You can give them to him, but they won't help him see,' Chief Jack cackled as he handed them back. 'He's been blinded by money!'

In that time-honoured tradition of hating your closest neighbours the most, the reviled settlement of Chief Kowiya turned out to be about three minutes' trundle down the hill. From the assorted references of Yaohnanen men, I'd come to expect some cross between Babylon, Pyongyang and the Gates of Hell. Whenever we heard a truck go by or saw a plane overhead, it was said that they belonged to Kowiya. Every localised gripe, from the bad road down to the coast to the skinniness of pigs, was traced to its source in the village of Yakel, presided over by its money-mad sorcerer-chief who'd blocked roads, broken the clay pipe of kastom and dealt with the devil. Only one story about Kowiya made men smile. And that was the time Kowiya had planted a fistful of dollars in the rich Tanna earth. He'd dug it up a year later, expecting compound interest, and found only a handful of caterpillar casings.

Nako walked ahead of me – once again in his Brisbane Girls' Grammar blazer, now with the collar turned up, like a craze that might have swept the Fifth Form in

1983. Perhaps he'd done it for protection against the wickedness of this greedy old chief. I was glad to get a chance to see Kowiya, but as I followed Nako's back through terraces of neatly tended yam gardens, I wondered why Imabel was still off the agenda. It was clearly the one place I needed to visit the most – having featured in the central myth that had caused so much confusion. Almost every day, I realised, I was promised a trip to this coastal Shangri-La. And every day, it didn't quite happen.

I was about to raise this, tactfully, with my guide, when we passed over a home-made cattle grid and Nako did something inexplicable. As I was crossing the precarious arrangement of rolling logs, he kicked one out of the way, so that I twisted my ankle. He helped me up again, but I was so astonished by his actions that it was some minutes before I could speak.

'Why did you do that?' I asked – baffled more than angry.

'You did fall,' he said philosophically.

'Yes, because you kicked the log out of the way.'

Nako shook his head slowly.

'Well, I saw it, Nako. It was a very odd thing to do.'

Nako looked down at my left foot. 'Now you have crashed the foot.' He sighed. 'I think you will not be able to go to Kowiya.'

I tested it. It was sore, but not unserviceable. 'I'll be all right.'

'It is hurt. You must go back to the village of my father.'

'No, I must not,' I said, deliberately walking on as quickly as I could. It had been a very odd exchange, quite without the rancour of our previous struggles, almost good-natured. But there was hardly anything friendly about what he'd done. If he'd done it.

We entered a sun-kissed little nakamal, screened off from the village by a tall, white fence. Once it became clear that we were in for one of the usual, limitless and inexplicable delays that were the island's speciality, I forced myself to stop thinking about the fall, and filled a half-hour making tiny, migraine-inducing jottings upon my dwindling supply of postcards. There'd been much to make notes on. And every answer brought in its wake a shoal of further imponderables. I felt it increasingly likely that the source of the myths had been the late Tuk Noao, but I wasn't sure if Chief Jack would take kindly to this finding, nor, yet, why he didn't know it already.

Nothing could quite explain his change of mood from outrage to whimsy, or why I'd still seen not a scrap of Philip worship going on. No shrines, no prayers, no hymns, no mention of shiploads of cargo. Philippism thrived in this place, I felt sure, but not in any form I recognised. And perhaps they didn't want me to recognise it. Was that why Nako had just tried to disable me?

Now Chief Johnson Kowiya came out, flanked by a cohort of buffed and befeathered braves in their penis sheaths. If we hadn't glimpsed people in T-shirts on our way in, I might have imagined they were a truly Stone Age people.

Chief Kowiya was older than Chief Jack, many times smaller, and the milky quality of his eyes suggested a pair of reading glasses from a Sydney pharmacist's were going to be of limited use. But I presented them, respectfully, and the old man sat opposite me, with his beefy lads behind. I kept thinking of Moore Marriott, the prematurely wizened actor who'd spent an entire career playing ancient codgers in Will Hay films. But Kowiya had also contributed to the BBC documentary that had first inspired me, speaking floridly about the life his people had lived before the coming of the white men. And one chunk of his speech had stuck in my memory all those years:

'Our time was not the same as your time. Our time was measured by the sun and the moon, through flowers, and the coming of birds and sea-worms. A man's age was not counted in years but in growth and ripeness. The vision of our past is beyond time. It is not a chronology, but a movement in space that comes and goes.'

Kowiya nodded as I recited his words back to him. 'That was in the time of nepro,' the old, gummy Chief confirmed. 'Before the whites came.'

I asked him about this word 'nepro', and he explained to me, in a quavering voice, that Tanna time was measured in cycles. Nepro was their Garden of Eden time, followed by numrukwen mo koyometa, when Tanna split into its two major lineages. After that came kaplelao, when people moved across the land as nomads; then noainesuio, when they began to fight with clubs. The list went on, until the tenth epoch, the modern age of politik – and judging by the look on his face as he mentioned it, Kowiya had no more enthusiasm for it than his enemy Chief Jack.

'You haven't learnt much, staying with them,' he said. 'You should have come here.' He cast a scornful glance at Nako, and added, 'How much is he charging you?'

I was a little distracted as the youngest of Kowiya's band, a rippling Ganymede with braided hair, began to prance around the nakamal with a bow and arrow, striking poses. But I regained enough composure to reply that Nako wasn't charging me anything. Chief Kowiya met this with a mocking laugh. 'But how much will he be charging the tourists?'

'What tourists?'

'Never mind,' Kowiya muttered. 'They'll be chased away again, as soon as they come. Chased down the hill to us.'

Yakel was mentioned in all the guidebooks as a place where visitors could see a traditional kastom village at work. And there was a strong whiff of the 'traditional-kastom-village-at-work' about all the chaps who'd accompanied the Chief into the nakamal. The braided youth stopped poncing about with his archery set and stood petulantly in the middle, as if awaiting further instructions.

'Take some pictures of him,' Kowiya urged.

I snapped one, to be polite, but it was no more than a tableau. The braids, I knew, were a traditional Tannese haircut, worn by men who'd assumed the memories of their ancestors along with their titles. It was possible to meet people on the island who said they'd been there when Captain Cook landed, and could give accounts that tallied with the historical record. Like a mnemonic, you went over each memory as you wound the braid, until your locks bounced and you'd become your ancestor. But I doubted, strongly, whether this lad now sulkily carving a souvenir war club in the centre of the nakamal had gone through such a process. He probably did modelling work in Sydney.

'Did they offer you any virgins?' Kowiya cracked. 'I tell you what. Take that boy's club off him, and get a picture of Philip holding it, and send it back to me. I'd like another ceremony.' The men behind him chuckled.

'Were you at the first one?' I asked, doggedly trying to ignore the nastiness.

'I don't remember,' Kowiya replied. 'It was 1978. Do you remember what you were doing in 1978? Are you a black man underneath, like Philip?' His acolytes cackled, and boosted by it, Kowiya raised his voice. 'Tell me – if you can afford the plane fare to Tanna, why can't Philip?' Roars of laughter.

We left soon after that, it being clear that Kowiya would tell me little of interest, and was only bothered about baiting his neighbours up the hill. Nako had remained stolidly silent throughout the rancorous little interview, and in spite of my throbbing foot, I felt strangely loyal towards him as we made our way home.

'They do not give to our hand one little small shell of kava,' he muttered incredulously.

'You're right. They didn't,' I said indignantly. This was extremely surprising behaviour. And even more surprising that I was so bothered. I'd somehow grown to love that daily scoop of space-spit, despite its taste and the terrible things it did to my insides. Overlooking the manner of its preparation, I loved the kava's chilly quietening creep from my oesophagus to my soul, and the still solemnity of the ceremony. If we could sell Tanna-strength kava in England, I thought, we'd bugger it up with acid jazz and even more acidic waitresses. But here they understood how to take it: talking softly, with your friends, by a fire, in the woods. And what an astonishing move it had been, for a man like Kowiya, to receive my gift, and proffer no kava in return.

'What did he mean about chasing away tourists?' I asked Nako as we neared the boundaries of Yaohnanen.

Nako shrugged. 'He is just an old man. Crazy.'

But Kowiya hadn't seemed crazy. Even if he had cataracts, his expression and his mannerisms were sharp as sharks. I was about to say this as we mounted the short earthen stairway to the nakamal, when Nako held me back.

A row was going on in the middle of the dusty space. Nako's fiercely bristled brother Kal was there, and Chief Jack, and a number of good ol' boys from the kava crew – fending off a heated deputation of unknown men. Not quite unknown men, in fact, because I recognised the slogan of a certain Canberra snack bar on the back of one of the invaders, and remembered when I'd first come across it. It was when we'd walked to Iatanas and Nako had been pushed into a bush.

'I have decided,' Nako said, trying to whisper urgently and sound casual at the same time, 'that we will go to see the photographs of the Prince Philip now.'

'But what's going on there?'

'It is very close,' Nako said, yanking fiercely at my bag, yet still trying to seem as if he was proposing nothing more pressing than a quiet pint on a Sunday afternoon. 'It is time you should see.'

And I wanted to see it, too; had been wanting and hinting ever since I first set foot on Tanna. So why now? What lay behind that argument in our village? Why had Kowiya been so rude to us? What did he mean about tourists? Deflecting, with the expert ease of a press officer, every one of my questions, Nako led me down a different bush path, past a field of bulls so bony they looked like coat hangers, then up a steep incline to a forlorn place of rocks. A prominent sorcerer was buried there, Nako told me, and in the middle of this jagged monument stood an affair on stilts, like something you might find in an adventure playground.

Nako climbed up the ladder of criss-crossing logs and went into a little booth, returning with two photographs of Prince Philip. He passed them over to me without a flourish or a trace of reverence. One, presumably the first, had been so ravaged by time and Tanna that only a ghostly trace of the image remained, fitting perhaps, for a spirit-Prince. The second, a simple head and shoulders, was dated 2000, and from Philip's eyes, I fancied, there flowed a veritable river of conflicting feelings. He looked stern and chief-like, exactly as his Tannese admirers would have wanted him to be. At the same time, there was a twinkle, and, perhaps, a hint of sheepishness, as if the gag had gone too far.

'What about the other one?' I asked, handling the dusty artefacts carefully. ' The one where he's holding the nalnal?'

'That is sent to another place,' Nako said.

'So your father sends them to different villages?' I hazarded. 'Like the kava branches – to open roads, make peace, that sort of thing?'

Nako considered this. 'Yes,' he answered, enigmatically. 'That sort of thing.'

'But why are these two here? Is this a tabu place for you?'

'This?' Nako glanced around him. 'No.'

'So there aren't any special ceremonies here?'

'Yes, they do kastom dancing here, all the time.'

'Kastom dancing for Prince Philip?'

'Prince Philip has never been to Tanna.'

I gripped the top of my scalp, to prevent it from coming off. 'I know that, Nako. I mean... Have you ever been inside a Christian church and seen what they do there? You know – singing songs. Asking God to help them...'

'No,' Nako declared proudly. 'That is Christians' fashion. We do not do.'

'So what do you do?'

'Christian men cannot see what we do.'

'But can I see?'

'Yes, you can see,' Nako said affably. 'Because I am the chief belong tok-tok which found you in Vila and brought you to this place, yes, you can see.'

'When?' I asked excitedly.

'All the time. Now. Come.'

With boyish eagerness I followed Nako out of the rock-strewn place, down another path and through thick, biting bush tunnels. We walked for a long time, and just as I was growing weak with thirst, a water tap appeared. Incredulous, filling my mouth with cold, liquid joy, I noticed traces of toothpaste around its base. This was our washing place, I realised, just a few feet away from the hut. I started to remark upon this to Nako, but he'd gone on ahead through the trees, and just as I turned the tap off, began to shout. I heard Kal talking, too, and the weaker, but somehow firmer voice of Chief Jack. I hastened down the muddy slope to find that our hut was wide open. Some of my things were scattered all around the place, dirty and crumpled.

'Was it a pig?' I asked, responding to the first, admittedly ridiculous image that formed in my head.

'Ol man long ples ia, ol i faet faetem tumas. Me wantem finis!' the Chief muttered. Everyone around here fights each other all the time. I want it to stop.

Then he seemed to emerge from his spiralling thoughts and noticed me. 'The police are looking for you.'

It seemed peculiarly Tannese, I thought, to claim to love peace and yet spend one's days steeped in faction fights and inter-village rivalries. And I couldn't help remembering that, when a real war came to this muddy, windy outcrop, the locals had loved it. In May 1942 the Americans arrived in planes – fulfilling Joe Nalpin's prophecy of eight months before. There was nothing supernatural about this. Port Vila, where Nalpin worked as a policeman, teemed with rumours of the unfolding war. The New Hebrides was the first French overseas territory to declare its support for De Gaulle and the Free French. The distant war was on everyone's lips, and from 1941 American planes had been spotted in the region.

Fears intensified after Pearl Harbour, and as the Japanese took control of New Guinea and the Solomon Islands, many white New Hebrideans fled to Sydney. Meanwhile the Americans set about building air bases, roads, wharves and a telephone system on Efate and Santo islands. From then until 1945 over 100,000 men were permanently stationed on the islands, and some half a million passed through, on their way to violent conflicts like Guadalcanal in the Solomons.

This required large amounts of local labour, and a thousand men from Tanna, including Jack Naiva, Kowiya and Tuk Noao, went to work on Efate. For many it was an opportunity to explore, to escape home and make money. But Tannese men went with a different sort of enthusiasm, because of Joe Nalpin's letter, and John Frum.

The Tannese were delighted by their contact with the Americans. Men interviewed in the 1980s by Lamont Lindstrom still spoke with misty eyes of their new employers. Thomas Nouar, of south-east Tanna, remembered complaining about the quality of the food they were given. He was astonished to find himself before two Big Men of the United States Army, one of whom was black, like himself. They listened to his complaint, and by that evening the diet had expanded to include rice, tinned meat and fruit. The accounts of other men describe the boundless generosity of the troops – doling out clothes, blankets, tinned goods, cigarettes. They noted with pride how Americans joined in their kastom dances, and showed them dances of their own. Even between men of high rank and themselves, they found a relationship of equality and friendliness.

Island pundits began to see clear similarities between America and Tanna – not just because of the presence of black troops. They analysed military praxis and organisation in terms of their own culture, concluding that various army ranks matched the 'canoe' system of village titles. This was a new trend in the ever-switching faces of white men. There'd been sympathetic souls before. But the Americans were more than friendly. They'd been prophesied, and they came. They stayed long enough to build relationships. It seemed as if a new type of white man had arrived.

The Japanese bombed Santo once, but there was only one casualty – a cow called Bossy. The main impact of the war was symbolic. Across the archipelago, people perceived a clear difference between the Americans and the only other foreigners with whom they were well acquainted: the British and French. America came to be seen as an ally, against the imperious colonial authorities, the planters, traders and missionaries.

This had an immediate kick-back into the John

Frum movement on Tanna, from where, in October 1942, Nichol frantically telegraphed the capital for troops. The stores were empty, as a result of religiously inspired spending sprees. Kava was being drunk all day, even by young boys. Few were attending church and school, and mission-created villages were being abandoned for scattered dwellings in the bush.

Fifty US Army soldiers were sent, under the command of Major Patton, though not the illustrious George Patton. They made for the village of Green Hill, where a prophet called Neloyiag had received visions of John Frum, a dark-skinned man with a rifle, who'd told him to build an airstrip.

Declaring himself John Frum's representative, and an ally of Rusefal (Roosevelt), the King of America, Neloyiag and his followers had cleared the bush and built a serviceable runway. This was what had happened on the main island of Efate, after all: people had built an airstrip, and soon after, American planes had appeared, laden with boots and guns, tinned food, tobacco, blankets. Now they were confident that would happen on Tanna, too.

And now, of course, the Europeans were really spooked. The natives getting smashed on kava and spending all their wages was one thing. But if black men could organise themselves enough to build an airstrip, then maybe they could organise themselves for other things, too. Like a rebellion.

Nichol arrested Neloyiag, and the troops seized all the weapons in the village. Major Patton delivered a speech, saying thanks, but America really didn't want another airstrip, as America wasn't coming to Tanna. He then issued a warning not to continue, by demonstrating the firepower of his army against an unoffending tree. Forty-six prisoners were shipped off to Port Vila.

Major Patton had come because of another fear: that the cult had been cooked up by Japanese traders on the islands, in order to ready the area for invasion. Intelligence reports eventually concluded that the Imperial Nippon Army had no designs on tiny, muddy, windswept Tanna. But elsewhere the Japanese had certainly played around with native cultists. On Karkar Island, in New Guinea, an officer with the invading forces told locals that they were the men they'd been 'expecting', and now they would help them to throw out the Europeans, and reward them with motor cars and houses. His speech was followed by a massive hand-out of loot.

Meanwhile Frum-like activities spread throughout the archipelago, to Pentecost and Malekula. Around one village on Ambrym, a militia appeared, run by men with the rank of captain and lieutenant. Upon entering the village, visitors had to state their name and business, just as one did on a US base. Newly widened roads were flanked by notices reading 'Halt!' and 'Stop!' There was other stuff, too: people watching out for a promised white cargo vessel, laden with goods, people talking to God on telephones made of tin cans. But with good reason, some observers wondered if all these cults were really proto-independence movements, ways of mobilising opposition to the whites, cloaked in a mystical disguise.

A few arrests – along with the failure of the prophecies to come true – caused the movement, in most cases, to peter out. But on Tanna it only gained momentum. The Stars and Stripes became a sacred emblem. American dog tags and uniforms became badges of membership.

Incidents continued. In 1951 excitement flared up over visions of a ghostly warship, piloted by a man called Captain World, and a friendly sailor, suspiciously like the bloke on the front of the Player's cigarette packet, called Jake Navy. In 1952, in a curious foreshadowing of the Prince Philip beliefs, a Tannese militiaman employed by the British administration informed his relations that the current British delegate, Mr Bristow, was a reincarnation of Noah. A very old Tannese legend, with echoes of myths found throughout Melanesia, said that two primordial brothers had been building a canoe on the seashore, when a wave swept away the older brother and the canoe. Since mission times this brother had been equated with Noah, who took all knowledge away with him, leaving his younger sibling, Man Tanna, poor and ignorant. A rumour spread that Noah had returned, disguised as a British civil servant, and was about to invite a warship to the island, to kick out the whites.

Something serious was happening here. The German anthropologist Eugen Fischer noted that colonised peoples will call upon any outside ally known to be different to their oppressors. In 1914, as Britain went to war, a cult in New Guinea had arisen, calling itself the German Wislun. Following the principle that one's enemy's enemy is one's friend, the Wislun awaited a massive cargo from Kaiser Wilhelm, and developed a secret language they said was German. Now the Tannese, caught up in their own struggles, and the eternal ping-pong match between different kinds of white men, had adopted America. It meant that, from now on, whenever new native movements emerged to fly the flag of kastom, help would be recruited from elsewhere.

In May 1957 an American warship, USS *Yankee*, called in at Tanna. In full naval uniform the ship's commander addressed John Frum leaders in the village of Ipeukel. He announced, on the authority of President Harry S. Truman, that no one in his country knew John Frum. He wasn't coming. And in any case, he didn't exist. But this, surely the oddest of all American naval missions, did not have the desired result. Cult leaders decided these were not real Americans. Once again the belief endured, whatever reality threw in its path.

In what was rapidly becoming the post-colonial world, the joint administration of the New Hebrides realised clamping down on the John Frum cult wouldn't work. So the exiled leaders were permitted to return, and the last deportee, Nakomaha, came back to his village of Ipeukel in January 1957. On 15 February red flags were raised on Ipeukel's dancing grounds, observed by two thousand followers, all expecting John Frum. He didn't come, but instead the two resident commissioners went to the village to demand that the flags be taken down. These were handed over without complaint, but to settle the matter without locking people up, it was decided to invite the US warship down to Sulphur Bay, on the south-east side of the island.

Two months after the *Yankee* had sailed away, a Tanna Army, headed by one 'General Nakomaha' emerged from the bush, where it had been drilling in secret for three months. Their faces were painted red. They sported white T-shirts bearing the words 'T.A – U.S.A.' and they held dummy bamboo guns. Several hundred young men marched in file towards Lenakel, the main town. Christians and whites were greatly alarmed. But the Tanna Army only expected to meet John Frum. Since he wasn't around, they dispersed without any violence.

The movement had become sizeable. When government repression ended in 1957, the island's 650 Catholics admitted they'd only been Christians in disguise, and went over to John Frum. The village of Ipeukel, at Sulphur Bay, became HQ for the movement. A former Presbyterian teacher and exiled Frumist, Tommy Nambas, became the figurehead, moulding the new cult out of the two models he knew well: the Church and the US army. Red crosses and hymn singing were used in worship. Missionaries were appointed to spread the word.

The ideology went on changing. When John Frum first appeared at Green Point, his message was like that of a cuddly suburban vicar – exhorting the audience to behave in a neighbourly fashion. Later the cult became more inner-city-radical-priest: a return to kastom values, the chucking out of the whites. Then it embarked upon a strange combination of material and mystical, with prophecies fixed upon the arrival of Americans with goods. Later America became the focus of hope, and it remains that way today, but as a sort of supernatural Peace Corps, sending skills, teaching them how to build factories and use computers. Given that this is what America and other nations actually do throughout the 'undeveloped' world, the expectations of the John Frum no longer seem that outlandish. The cult also brings in a tidy amount of revenue from tourism, ensuring that John Frum villages often have better access to transport, water and healthcare. In that light, it's worth asking if it hasn't, in fact, really succeeded.

I still didn't understand where Yaohnanen fitted in, though. Frum worship, though headquartered in the east of the island, was everywhere, and, as with Chief Jack's outburst outside our invaded hut, the name of 'John' popped up in almost every conversation. So why had this village gone its own way, rejecting John Frum for a god who didn't bring in the tourist dollars, only ridicule and hostility from its neighbours, and the world at large? My time on the island was coming to a close. But I still had much to find out.

CHAPTER SEVEN

A Bigfella Tok-Tok Where It Is Decided That Nobody Has Really Done Anything Wrong Except Me

KAVA dreams that night: I saw a totem pole, with a stern-faced Muppet on top. I knew he was the god Kalbaben, though, and he was pointing me towards a ravine, in a modern, sky-scrapered city which I knew to be called 'Canada'. Crowds were flocking to this smoking gully in the city, like Ground Zero, a space where a building should have stood. I peered over the sides to see a crashed aeroplane, picked over by police in fluorescent waistcoats.

When I awoke, to the crowing of cocks and the grunting of bush pigs, I remembered where this symbol of a crashed aeroplane had come from. Back in England, trying to get my hands on any literature on cargo cults, I'd tracked down a book entitled, handily enough, *Cargo Cult*. It turned out to contain a singularly tiresome kind of beat poetry, and nothing about cargo cults at all. But the image on the cover was striking: an airliner, sprawled like a drunk at the bottom of beetling cliffs. With a mystic fogginess typical of my first waking moments, I fancied the dream was telling me something. Kalbaben was ordering me away from his island. Before it was too late.

So powerful was this impression that I told Nako, who was, unexpectedly, sitting on the floor with a lump of lit charcoal in the end of his pipe. He must have been inhaling nothing but pure carbon monoxide, and perhaps that accounted for his reaction. 'I will erect the truck,' was all he said, when I'd been expecting a long lecture on the subject of why whatever I wanted could not be done, for secret, tribal reasons I was not entitled to ask. Then again, I hadn't even been expecting Nako to be in the hut that morning. It wasn't his usual way at all.

'I don't want to go right now. There's still things I have to do. But I think I should leave tomorrow.'

'I can erect the truck in a half of an hour,' Nako said, tapping the glowing coal out of his pipe. 'It will not take until tomorrow.'

'I don't want the truck to be erected today, Nako. I want to go tomorrow.'

'You are sure?' Nako asked, standing up.

'Sure.' On hearing this, Nako spat moodily on the ground. Why was he so keen for me to go now? 'Perhaps, seeing as it's going to be my last day,' I added, 'we could go to Imabel.'

Nako shook his head. 'Cannot go. My father has spoken along the road.'

'What has he spoken?'

'A big tok-tok here in the nakamal of the village belonging to me. All the men of the places around this place will come.'

'What's the reason for it?'

'Reason belonging to this place,' Nako said grimly, opening the door of the hut, but still spitting inside it.

'Is it something to do with the argument? And the police?'

'Not these,' he said, leaving and kicking the door shut behind him. But I suspected otherwise. And perhaps he was right to try and hustle me out of the area, with the police, inexplicably, on my trail, and gangs of furious men making daily protests at our front door. Perhaps he was only thinking of my safety, or negative consequences from the capital if a visitor came to harm in a kastom area.

When I stepped out into the village, I found old Chief Jack in a nail-biting mood, pacing the ground before his hut, in a long pair of khaki shorts and a mauve batwing jumper. Kal and Nako stood with him, nodding gravely as their father shot curses into the sky and issued edicts with a flung-out finger. So great was the Chief's distraction that, as I approached, he broke off speaking and returned to his hut without the slightest sign of recognition. I was baffled and hurt.

Nako came up and said that, for reasons withheld, I couldn't stay in the village for a while. I should come with him, he said, and take a look at the schoolhouse. The men had started work today. So we walked past Iatanas, home of the Missionary and the multi-coloured dervish team, and past a paddock containing a short, fat horse, down to a wide, flat meadow. What I saw there filled my eyes with tears.

My favourite film is *Witness*, where a tough city cop finds a purer, warmer way among the backward-looking, Bible-devoted Amish. The scene where Harrison Ford helps a village build a barn – to a backing track of suitably inspiring strings – ranks, for me, among the most beautiful of all moving images. It still couldn't compare to this.

There were men of Yaohnanen there – and of Iatanas, of Ielgis, Ioknaauka, Iakukak and Iapnamal. Every tongue-tying village name of Tanna had ambassadors there, sawing, hammering, binding, weaving under the watery morning sun. The air almost stung with their sweat, and they sang a whooping, swooping field holler as the schoolhouse slowly rose in their hands. The Freddie Mercury man – he who'd been haranguing the prayer meeting in Iatanas – was first to see me, and he let out a great cry of greeting. Jimmy Yasu took it up, and the whole beavering team atop the log frame began to wave and grin. I scanned the scene, somewhat anxiously, for a sign of my friend Siyaka. I could almost not bear the idea of him combined with heights, unstable buildings and saws. But oddly, he wasn't there.

Shouts came from behind me, and I saw, on the other side of the bush path, another party working on a series of squat, conical reed huts.

'What are they?' I asked Nako.

'For the visitors,' Yasu said, appearing with a damp handshake. 'Don't worry, they will be ready in time.'

'In time for what?'

The women, too, were at work there, knitting together the latticed walls from flat, flexible reeds. Nako ignored my question and went to take a new-born baby from a young girl, cradling it in the crook of his arms, where it nuzzled contently.

'The baby of Kal,' he said. 'It is a girl.'

The baby which had been born – not burnt, as I'd misheard that night. I looked again at the girl who'd been holding the baby, suddenly realising she was Kal's wife, transformed again into a pretty teenager.

'You have spoken the name on the child,' Nako said to me, holding her up.

'What do you mean?'

'You have put the name,' he clarified, although it didn't exactly clarify anything.

'Her name is Matthew,' Yasu added, bathing me in his trademark spooky gaze. 'Because of you.'

'Well. That's … that's very kind of everyone,' I stammered.

'Not kind,' Yasu said, his eyes widening to such a point that they seemed to take over the sky. 'You put the name upon this place as well. That's why they chose it to build the school. It's called London,' he said.

'Must have been named by the missionaries, eh?'

'No. It was always called London, long before any white men came here. Before John. Before Americans. Before the missionaries and Captain Cook. Because of you.'

'I don't come from London,' I said nervously.

'Yes,' Yasu replied, as if he hadn't heard, or words had ceased to matter. 'We know you come from a village called Southport. You told Siyaka. Southport means south of Port Vila, and Tanna is south of Port Vila, so you see, Matthew, your whole life has been leading up to this moment.'

Yasu – the combination of his saucer-sized eyes, his solitary dreadlock and his sinister patter – was beginning to unnerve me now. So, too, was everyone else gathered in that sunny field – they'd all stopped working and were beaming at me, silently, expectantly.

'I think I'll just go and have a sit-down over there,' I said brightly.

'Three of the girls in the village have stopped menstruating,' Yasu called after me. 'Soon there will be more of them, so that no more babies can be born anywhere. It's because all the old people are going to become young again, just like it says in that letter you brought.'

'Right.'

I turned back to face Yasu, whose face bore that luminous expression of people who belong to a very new Church. 'It's not a letter, Yasu. It's just a…'

'Prophet Fred wants to meet you,' he interrupted. 'He's been having dreams about you.'

Normally an invitation to meet someone called Prophet Fred would have been very appealing to me. But I'd had enough. I'd had so much, in fact, that some moments after receiving Yasu's last piece of good news, I found myself crashing down the Tanna slopes on a barely traceable bush path, with his voice ringing out behind me. 'Matthew! You go where now?' I didn't know where I was going, and I wouldn't have answered him even if I had. I just wanted to get away – quickly. I didn't want people having dreams about me. I didn't want people believing there was any truth to the stories I'd been reading out, or that I was anything other than a person trying to write a book. And why did they? What had I said or done?

I felt safer as I went deeper into the dark, encircling world of creeper vines, farther and farther away from that smiling crowd in the sunlit meadow. They'd send someone after me, for sure. They'd want to know why the Englishman had dashed away from them into the bush. If they asked, I decided, then I'd tell them. 'You're making me rather scared,' I'd say.

I stumbled through a series of dimming glades, first

coming across a pig with an aggrieved expression, and then an odd little structure made of canes, which could have been a discarded item of Tannese garden- ware, or something of profound and sinister religious significance. There was light somewhere in front, and pushing aside with my head the outer branches of some shrub composed of steel needles, I realised I was on the lip of an unfamiliar nakamal. Meeting grounds meant roads, and my heart lifted. I could still myself in the dusty sunshine for a while and head back by safer means.

I stepped out bravely, only to bring my foot down on a great quantity of thin air, cunningly covered by weeds. With a strangled cry I found myself at an inter- esting angle, almost, but not exactly upside down. It was from this unhappy vantage point, scratched and dazed, that I realised the meeting ground was occu- pied. There was a flat-bed truck, new and shiny, and with one foot on the gleaming running board, a man in a pale-blue tunic and navy-blue trousers. Opposite him was a taller individual in a pressed and vigorously patterned shirt. They seemed to be scanning the area – no doubt because of the cry that had recently issued from the brambles. As the blue man turned, I caught a gleam of metal on his belt.

A policeman. And yesterday, after that strange, angry business in the village, after visiting the high, windy place where the royal photographs rested at the side of a dead sorcerer, what had Chief Jack said? 'Man belong polis em i look long you.' The police are looking for you.

A radio crackled inside the cab and the man leant in to check it. He was plainly on duty. And looking for someone. I had nothing to fear, though, did I? I had permission to be here, and the schoolhouse being erected just a few hundred yards away was testimony to the deal I'd brokered back in Port Vila. I could walk out there, conscience clear, and greet him.

I ducked back into the bushes. The pig was there, with a cool, weary look on its face. Some Tannese pigs are so revered that they are treated as chiefs, and given a red stripe down their noses. This one seemed to be in training for that moment.

I sat forlornly in among the prickles for a while, until the massed forces of the Tanna constabulary got into their truck, retuned the radio to Celine Dion and drove away. Shortly afterwards the remaining man stared into the bushes and ordered me out.

'Why are you hiding in the garden, Matthew?'

'It's not a particularly good garden,' I observed, picking thorns from my forearms as I stepped into the light. 'Maybe you don't do all that much gardening, really?'

Lomakom simply snorted. 'Maybe you've done something you are ashamed of, and that's why you are hiding?'

I'd been in countries where the police force had guns and sometimes used them without thinking. That, I said, was the only reason I'd been hiding.

'Police?' Lomakom queried. 'You thought he was a policeman. Ha! He was from the government. The poor people here have no money for the Independence Day celebrations, so I am making the government give us a bullock to eat.' A politician to the last, Lomakom used every exchange to advertise his achievements. Now he began to smile. 'But you are afraid of the police? Interesting. That the man from Buckingham Palace should be afraid of the police, so afraid he hides in this garden and covers himself in…'

I followed his disdainful look to the bottoms of my trousers, which were plastered in fresh pig shit. 'Hang on,' I exclaimed, suddenly recalling his last words. 'I haven't come from Buckingham Palace.'

Lomakom was about to offer some gloating comment on this matter when Kal sprinted into the arena.

'Come on,' he said to me brusquely. 'Don't talk to him.' He made to take my arm.

'Fuck off,' I bridled. I felt fourteen again, being flushed by prefects from the smokers' dens of the nearby park. I shouldn't have sworn at Kal, of course. No one on Tanna swore. They were so prudish that they went swimming with their hands over their cocks – something Golovnin had noted about them, long before Christian missionaries could have introduced any notions of bodily shame. But my response caused Kal to step back a little.

'You have to come now,' he said, more gently. 'The tok-tok will begin soon, and my father wants you to be there, because he will be giving out the pipes.'

'All right,' I said testily. 'But don't grab me, and don't tell me who I can't talk to.'

'See you soon!' Lomakom called out, cattily, as we left. For the most part we walked in silence, until we were almost by my hut.

'We have to wait here,' Kal said sullenly.

So we sat on the grassy verge, and when the silence between us became unbearable, I made some tiny notes on a postcard. During this process Kal cleared his throat and tapped me on the arm.

'Why do you write on those pictures?'

I tried to find some hostile motive behind this question, but couldn't find one. 'They're postcards,' I said eventually.

'What are postcards?'

'When people visit a place, they buy a picture of it, and they send it to their friends, to show them where they've been.'

Kal gently took the cards from me and sifted through them. 'But we don't have buildings like this on Tanna.'

'They're from Australia. I was going to send them to Prince Philip, but then I forgot my notebook, you see, so I'm just using them for notes.'

Kal stared at the Sydney Harbour Bridge thoughtfully, clicking his tongue against his teeth. Abruptly, he handed them back and sprang up. He looked like he was about to do fifty star-jumps. 'You saw my new daughter in the field?'

'Yes, I did,' I answered warily. This was the longest conversation I'd ever had with the man, and somewhere, underneath the stares and the gleaming biceps, was a strange sense of Kal being friendly. 'I was glad you gave her my name.'

He looked at the ground. 'You know, on Tanna, all of our names belong to somebody who came before?'

'Yes, I'd heard that.'

'And when we put the name on them, they do not just take the name, but the memories of that person as well?'

'Yes…' I said, wondering where all this might be leading. Was I going to have to donate a few memories to this little girl? I couldn't, in that instant, think of any that would suit. Stealing a royal teapot from a jumble sale? No, that wouldn't do.

'Not just the memories, but the soul of that person,' Kal said gruffly. 'Already my wife is saying that the girl has very weak eyes.'

'Oh dear…'

'Yes. She has large ears and weak eyes and feet that are not straight and she is sick all the time. So I think we will not call her Matthew any longer, if you don't mind.'

Kal began to make an odd, creaking sound, as if the lower part of him was slowly being pushed into the top half, and already certain compressed fluids were starting to froth from his eyes and mouth. It was only when he delivered an almighty slap to my back that I realised what was going on. Kal had made a joke.

I was the brunt of it, of course, but it was quite a decent effort, and I had a feeling it was almost kindly meant. It was, at any rate, such a shock to encounter humour from the bristle-rimmed lips of Tanna's angriest drill instructor that I found myself laughing as well. I was still laughing when Siyaka came charging down the path with a slowly disintegrating bundle of firewood. This genial bear of a man – today sporting the sort of bright-green felt waistcoat favoured by folk musicians – was just the sort to appreciate a good gag. But he shot me a disgusted look and pushed past me, leaving a trail of sweat and twigs. I was utterly stunned, and allowed Kal to lead me, cow-like, back to the village for humiliations even harder to bear.

The nakamal roared with tok-tok, tink-tink, spitting, smoking, chewing, men and boys and dogs. But as I walked into it, the noise died away. As with the circumcision ceremony, the menfolk had grouped themselves by village around the circular space, each village lighting its own smoky fire so that, with the silence, the place took on some faintly awful air, like the scene of an impending sacrifice. In a row cutting across the top of the circle sat Yaohnanen, like a panel of judges, or possibly, the accused. Kal led me to a spot in this line and I sat on the earth, feeling the gaze of a multitude.

The clay pipes were laid out on a mat in front of Chief Jack and he rose to deliver a lengthy oration. Each separate group around the place then sent forth a spokesman, to receive an allotted number of pipes and then deliver a further speech of their own. One – memorably adorned with a T-shirt enquiring 'How Do You Like Your Eggs In the Morning?' – gave a song instead of a speech, and this was received with a shocked roar of appreciation, because the mood had been tense until then. The tension rapidly climbed again, though, as four more speeches followed.

Each spokesman rose to say his part, and no one interrupted. Tok-tok was sacred on Tanna. They held ceremonies to mark a child's first word; and no man was a Big Man if he couldn't deliver a good speech. Good, in the first instance, meant long, but it also implied wit and insight, an exhaustive knowledge of local history and founding myths. In the Christian villages, Sunday services were day-long affairs as all the Big Men, and those who aspired to the title, took to the pulpit for an hour or more apiece. To talk was to do: a road, campaigned for by a prominent local leader, was described as the road that the Chief *spoke*. To be silent was to be 'yapu' – weak, sick, exhausted.

The final speaker was a thin, baleful streak, whose scrubby moustache and military blouson reminded me of someone from the world of TV sitcoms, possibly Blakey, the morose, officious senior ticket inspector in *On the Buses*. He delivered his tok-tok in Nauvhal, directly to my face, rather in the manner of a complaint, and at the end, I was called upon to answer him.

'I don't know what he said.'

'Say you don't know,' Nako offered shiftily. I noticed beads of sweat forming on his brow.

'But what don't I know?'

In answer, Nako would only titter, so I was compelled to rise to my feet and tell my dolorous interlocutor that I didn't know what I didn't know. He sat down, justifiably unsatisfied, only to be replaced by someone who looked extremely pleased with himself.

'Good morning, Matthew,' Lomakom boomed, revolving his head around the arena so that his words reached every ear. 'I should like it if you would explain some things, please, because some people here are rather confused.'

From my seat on the ground, I said I would be glad to assist. 'STAND UP!' roared the entire crowd.

'I said I would be glad to assist,' I said, standing up again.

'Thank you,' Lomakom purred. He paused, pointedly waiting for something. 'Sit down then.'

Knees creaking, I sat back down as local politician Lomakom paced the arena, like an actor giving the final performance of a long career. 'Please tell us,' he asked, 'if Prince Philip sent you to Tanna.'

Was that really what people thought? I got to my feet. 'No.' I sat down again.

'Did he give you money, to build up the kastom school, and make a tourist village?'

'No. Why are you asking that? Who said that?'

'STAND UP!!'

'Look – does anyone mind if I just stand up or sit down but not both?' I pleaded, staggering to my feet again, and seeing little sparks at the corners of my vision.

'It is not our way, Matthew, but if that is your wish, then you may.' Lomakom smiled me a smile that was like having your inner thigh unexpectedly rubbed by your girlfriend's dad. 'So to be clear, you have no connection to Prince Philip?'

'No!' I protested, glancing to Nako for support. He was gazing intently at an insect. 'I'm just a writer.'

'I have met these writers in Port Vila,' Lomakom observed, mock-thoughtfully. 'And they write things down, all the time, in little notebooks. But you don't have a notebook. All you do is write postcards. Like tourists do. Because, you are, in fact, just a tourist, aren't you? You are not from Prince Philip and you are not a writer. You may sit down.'

'But I'm…'

'Sit down.'

I obeyed him, my face burning, as the Blakey looka-like stood once again and delivered a further bout of plaintive drizzle in my direction. I asked if he could say it in Bislama, but for some reason he would not. Once more I looked across at Nako for help, but he seemed lost in a misery of his own. In despair I invited Lomakom to interpret for me, but he simply rubbed his chin, and said this confirmed my identity as a tour-ist. A writer would have bothered, surely, to learn the language of the place he was writing about.

Nako was called to the stand next, and my tiny vo-cabulary was soon exhausted by the lengthy, quick-fire interrogation that followed. All I could tell for certain was that Nako wasn't too happy.

'He is saying Nako should not have gone around all the villages misleading people.' I smelt fuel, and turned to see the Missionary kneeling behind my shoulder with his usual greasy grin.

'Around all the villages?'

'Yes,' he nodded happily. 'He has been going to a different place every morning, very early, and reading those stories of yours, and telling people Prince Philip has sent a man here to tell them all the things that are going to happen.'

Which explained Lomakom's line of questioning. Explained, too, where Nako had been every morning. Why he'd wrestled custody of the stories from me. Why he'd hustled me away from every conversation I'd begun without his supervision. And God only knew what sort of things he'd been promising.

'Iakukak, Ielgis, Iatanas...' I heard Lomakom reciting, counting off the villages on his fingers. I listened carefully.

'Did he mention Imabel?' I asked the Missionary.

'I don't think Nako went to Imabel,' he said. 'But wherever he went, he said Prince Philip had given you money to build up the school, and there might be money to build a place like the Lovely Bungalows, for the tourists.'

I took a deep breath. 'Right. And what was that old man with the moustache saying?'

The Missionary blushed and giggled, and then Lomakom went full throttle for his summing up – an impressive affair, even if delivered in a language I couldn't understand. It pounded mercilessly upon the weakened form of Nako like foreign gunfire, crackling with insults and the pride of a righteous accuser. As it ended, the nakamal ripped apart with applause.

'What did he say?'

'He said Nako was sent away for being blinded by money, always trying to make more from the tourists who used to come here. He said that's why Yaohnanen lost them. And that's why he came back, with you.'

A wind ruffled my sooty hair, and with it came a memory of Kirk's words, in the cooked meats aisle of a

Sydney supermarket. 'You're going to be Nako's ticket.'
That didn't mean it was as simple as that. Or that Lomakom, from the mission-educated, English-speaking
Vanuaaku Pati, was giving an unbiased view of a kastom
opponent. But it gave me some clues.

A dance followed, and another musical number
from the bloke in the Dean-Martin-song-lyric T-shirt,
and then pots of food were taken out by the Yaohnanen
men and placed in front of each village. A mingling
affair then took place, and I observed Nako passing
among the crowds, shaking hands and joking, as if
he'd been the hero of the hour. No one seemed to be
nursing much of a grudge – Nako even swapped a rela-
tively spite-free sentence or two with Lomakom. It was
almost as if, in the act of holding a tok-tok, the matter
had been resolved. Nako had been trying it on, been
hauled up and held to account, and now everyone was
happy. A few days ago a sizeable chunk of them had
been expecting the return of an exiled god, the dawn
of a new paradise with eternal life and mature kava
springing out of the ground. Now, it seemed, they'd
been mistaken. But shit happened. Everything was OK.

Almost OK. Nobody came to shake my hand – not
even the Missionary. As I wandered around, the crowds
parted like curtains onto a painful apprehension of the
truth. They blamed me. Nako, one of their own, had
just been doing what every self-respecting Man Tanna
was obliged to do. With no rigid ladders of pig-based

social progress to climb, every soul on the island had the right, opportunity and duty to establish himself as someone of clout. Some did it through visions and dreams, some through politics, some through money. In hitching himself to my wagon, Nako had been having a stab at all three, and this, perhaps, had been his undoing. But no one blamed him for having a go. At me, though, his instrument and agent, they looked askance. You should have known better, they seemed to say, with their averted glances and their turned shoulders. You misled us; he didn't.

I felt a tug at my arm, and with it, a surge of relief. Thank God someone here had a kind word for me. I turned and received a damp blast of decaying teeth from Blakey, who'd sought me out especially in my lonely corner. 'I don't understand you,' I said. 'I don't understand.' He drifted away, and continued to cast me baleful looks from his corner.

As I sat alone on the log they'd called my bush armchair in the happier times, I saw Yasu and Siyaka in the crowd. They'd not even gone near me. I knew why I'd dreamt of a crashed airliner now; it was the collapse of my dreams, the dashing of hope on the rocks of reality, the shattering of fragile friendships. You will be broken in this place – that was what Nako had said, just after we landed. And he hadn't meant the luggage cart at all. The log creaked a little and I saw Chief Jack seating himself delicately at my side.

'Can I have a look at your engine?' he asked unexpectedly.

I handed over my voice recorder, and showed him
how to use the various functions. He played a little section back, smiling as a man's voice came from the tiny
speaker. 'I know him,' he said. 'Remi from Iatanas.'

'I said I'd give you this machine when I left. Would
you like it?'

He shook his saintly head. 'America has a lot of
these machines. And still they can't find one old sorcerer, hiding in a cave.'

'What sorcerer?'

'He's a very wise-looking man, very tall, I think, with
a long beard and a big nose.'

'Do you mean Osama bin Laden?'

'I don't know his name. But he wants to take all the
kerosene from America, so that they will be in darkness.' He shrugged. 'They just need some men from
Tanna to help them, just as we did in Wolwatu. We will
find this kleva with some leaves and some stones...'
He fell silent for a moment, then handed the machine
back. 'What did you find?' he asked.

Perhaps Chief Jack was handing me a chance to
redeem myself. If I'd found the source of those missing
myths, all might be forgiven. But I hadn't. Everything I
had discovered pointed in the direction of an uncom-
fortable truth. That the Chief's friend, Tuk Noao, had
had visions of his own, and shared them with a white

man, but not with his fellow seers in the nakamal. I wondered how to put it – and, if, indeed, I should.

At that moment, as so often happened on Tanna, a molecule-sized miracle occurred, as Daniel – he of the inscribed gangsta trousers – strode into the nakamal and directly up to us. He looked breathless and elated.

'Have I missed it?'

'Not quite,' I said. Here was my one hope. If this boy from Imabel knew the stories, and Nako hadn't taken his one-man roadshow there, then perhaps some renegade group of Philippists had formed. Perhaps Imabel was the transgressor and perhaps, in demanding recompense, the Chief could brush aside the recent ignominies visited upon his own community. 'Tell the Chief here – where did you get those stories about Prince Philip from?'

Daniel – whose modishly skewed cap declared its owner to be an Original GangStarr – murmured a few words to the Chief. The old man sat back, folding his leathery arms with a not too satisfied expression on his face. 'What did you tell him?'

'I got 'em from that bloke over there,' Daniel said, pointing to Nako, who was now cheerfully accepting some stick tobacco from Lomakom. 'I stayed the night with some blokes in Ielgis last week. And this bloke came over in the morning, starts reading these stories out.'

'But … but you knew them so well.'

'Yeah. Well.' He sucked his teeth thoughtfully. 'People have got good memories here.'

He recognised some muckers in the throng, clapped me on the back and wheeled across the nakamal, leaving me alone again with Chief Jack.

'I don't know where the stories came from,' I said in the end. 'Sorry.'

'I know.'

I blinked in surprise. 'Do you?'

'I expect it was Tuk Noao,' the Chief said casually. 'He was the Voice of the Canoe back in those days. He was a big talker and a thinker. Not like me. And, of course, he spent a lot of time with your friend Cook Gavman.'

'But…'

'Perhaps it's because you write things down and put them inside little engines that you don't know how our stories are. Cook Gavman understood, I think. But he had a job to do, so…' The Chief shifted so that he was facing me. 'Every one of our stories is like a stone thrown into a pond. It sends out ripples, getting bigger and bigger all the time, so that in the end you can only see the last of the ripples and not the stone or the place where the stone went into the pond. You see?'

'Erm…'

'Yes, the stone of Prince Philip landed here,' he said, patting the log. 'But then the ripples went all across the island. They are still going on now, further and further

234

out all the time. There will always be more stories, so it makes no sense to take this one or that one and put it on a piece of paper and say this is the story, and it came from here. That's something they do in Australia and London.'

'But you were angry when I read them out to you. You told me to go round all the other villages, and ask them about the stories. Don't you remember?'

'Yes, I was angry,' the Chief said. 'Because when you came, you made the tamafa and you looked at the mountain and you brought us pipes, and I thought, you must come from Philip. But then I realised you didn't understand anything. If you'd understood any-thing, I don't think you'd have come here with stories on pieces of paper, because you'd have known that our thing isn't like that, it's alive and it's moving.'

'But you said you wanted us all to drink kava, so the kava would give us an answer.'

'I wanted the kava to give an answer to you,' the Chief said. 'Not to anyone else. And I didn't tell you to go round the other villages. You said it was something you could do – and I said that if you went, you might learn something. That was what I hoped. But you never did.'

'Learn what?'

'We don't sing songs to Prince Philip. We don't go into a special house. We don't have … sticks like this' – he made the sign of the cross with his hands – 'or dances or anything like that. You know why?'

'No.'

'Christians do that. John Frum people do it, with their American flags and their wooden rifles and marching. And what happens? Has Jesus Christ come yet? Has John? Everything they do to bring them here – it just blocks the road.'

'So what do you do?'

'We walk slowly. We work in the gardens. We drink kava. We keep it in our hearts. And what happens? Prince Philip sends us photographs and letters. We have built a road, and because we continue to do it our way, the kastom way, and not the way of the Christians and the John people, one day men from Tanna will meet him. You will be a gate for this to happen. It will happen through you.'

'And what will happen when they meet him?' I asked carefully. 'Will he give them things?'

'We want *him*. Because he belongs to Tanna and this is his home. If I took your arm away,' the Chief concluded, 'you would want it back, wouldn't you?'

I nodded numbly, having learned more in that last minute than in weeks of perplexing interviews and power struggles. But that, too, seemed to slot perfectly into what the Chief had been saying. Strive too hard and you block the road. To succeed, stop trying. And how typical, too, that this phenomenon so often described as a cargo cult should have no interest in cargo, and pride itself on being entirely unlike a cult. It was pure tink-tink – an idea, a spirit, that would be sullied if they fleshed it out with rituals and hymns.

That, too, was something springing straight from the volcano-shaken soils of this remarkable place. Unlike the other islands of the archipelago, Tanna's material culture was sparse. You didn't find the elaborate headdresses, or carved canoes, or vivid bark cloths that made other islands in the archipelago so noteworthy. You found muddy, ragged villages and villagers shivering in the T-shirts richer countries had no use for. But, in turn, the people of Tanna had no use for those riches. What they had use for could not be apprehended by the mere acts of looking and touching, but absorbed, slowly, through the business of waiting there in its nakamals, drinking its kava, soaking in through your skin the secrets of its endless toktok and tink-tink.

Chief Jack patted my leg. 'We will take kava soon.' And before he padded off, to organise the mass scrubbing, chewing, spitting operation required to send a couple of hundred souls spinning into space, he added, 'I will get them to prepare a big root for you to take back home.'

'That's really kind. But I won't be allowed.'

The Chief cocked his head. 'What? Who will block it?'

'It'll be taken off me at the airport. By the Customs people.'

Chief Jack tutted sadly. 'That's dreadful. Kastom people have a whole island full of kava for themselves, and yet they go to the airport to take it off the tourists!'

'No, Chief, not kastom people. I meant…'

'It's nothing but greed!' the Chief declared. 'That's why Philip's road is still blocked. When you get home, I want you to write that on one of your postcards and send it to him. Tell him we will do our part, here, but he must do his. He must go to the Parliament, and tell the men there to join him. In a war against greed.'

CHAPTER EIGHT

The Englishman Who Travelled Ten Thousand Miles to Find A Cargo Cult That Wasn't Interested in Cargo and Wasn't a Cult, Either

WITH Nako and Kal in the cab beside me, we drove to the coast, passing through a number of the villages I'd visited on my wanderings. On a tight bend, two men stood aside to let us pass – one reaching in to shake my hand, the other settling for a sullen glare. That was Siyaka, in a nondescript light-grey T-shirt, as if all his wackier costumes had been discarded along with his hopes. We passed him and I turned back, just in time to see him lift his hand for a vague, brief, uncertain gesture that might have been a wave, or a 'fuck you'. Turning back, I wished curses upon Nako's oblivious head. If anyone was to blame for Siyaka's coldness, it was him. And if any of the mission's failures mattered to me, it was that one.

We halted just outside Lenakel, where the street of churches still offered a cocktail of coffee mornings and apocalyptic prophecy. Kal disappeared into a roadside hut for a few moments.

'What's Kal doing?'

Nako shrugged, using just his thumbs, a cold, diffident gesture, expressing, very clearly, the point that I was of no more use to him. I made a long 'ffff' sound through my teeth, to which he offered no further response. It was a good job I was going home.

Further along the road we met a smartly dressed young man who said he was a policeman. He leant into the cab and showed me his ID card. As he exchanged some words with Kal, I found myself fantasising about a kastom-based TV cop show, with weekly mysteries based on myth theft and mischievous rain magic. They could even call it *Tanna Law*.

'You were supposed to register with us at the police station if you wanted to stay here for a long time,' the policeman said. 'That's why I came to find you other day.'

'Oh,' I said, wondering if this was a preamble to the extraction of cash. 'Sorry.'

'That's all right,' he said, grinning. 'You'll know next time.'

I shot Nako a look, a look, I hoped, communicating the point that if I ever came back, it wouldn't be with him. He had the decency to look away.

At the airport, something was blocking the runway, so we had to wait. Nako and Kal sat grimly on the grass beside me, muttering in their mother tongue, treating me to monosyllables. I'd told them they didn't need to wait, but Kal had said, rather disarmingly, that they liked to see the planes take off. That crumb of charm aside, he remained as sour and watchful as he'd ever been. Nako just ignored me.

Finally the runway was cleared, and a man in an improbably elaborate uniform came striding around the little field next to the terminus building, instructing us all to line up inside. I stood, shouldered my bag and stared Kal in the eye, determined to do this with chilly dignity.

Suddenly he lunged at me. I stepped back in alarm, but too late. He grabbed me, squeezing the breath from my bones. I expected the second act to follow soon – the kick to the shins, the jab to the solar plexus. He pushed me away from him, both hands upon my shoulders, an inscrutable expression on his face. A punch to the jaw? Or would he surge forward with his forehead, that gesture known in my part of the world as a Bootle Handshake?

'I like you,' he announced, glaring all the while. 'Please come again. Thank you.' His stern moustache suddenly curled into a grin as he pumped my hand. Relief rushed through me. It was another of his gags. I grinned back as Kal reached in his pocket and produced a little package, wrapped in newspaper.

'I hope it's not kava,' I said, continuing the wind-up. 'Because you know, I really don't like that stuff.' I made a face. Kal's smile vanished.

'It's not kava. It's our island tobacco.' He handed me the package. I blushed.

'Thank you, Kal,' I said feebly, sheepishly, to his departing back. I couldn't help stuffing things up, it seemed, even unto the very last minutes.

I lugged my dusty bags to the check-in stand with confused feelings. Had my whole visit been like that last moment, I wondered, a clumsy clown of a bloke, blundering into that frail, delicate mountain society, crashing its taboos and shaking it with my questions and my assumptions? Or had I been used by them, a handy dupe for their never-ending politicking, a tool in both senses of the word? Both were probably true. And both, I would discover, as I soothed my damaged soul in the library at the Vanuatu Cultural Centre, were very typical of Tanna's ongoing relationship with white men. That includes its relationship with Philip.

The final chapter, and the final spark to fire up the worship of the Duke of Edinburgh in Yaohnanen, began with a telegram from Tanna to Buckingham Palace. It wasn't the Tannese who'd sent it, but one Antoine Fornelli, a Corsican former Foreign Legionnaire and plantation owner, whose new, self-conferred job title was King of Tanna. A similar telegram had gone to the French President, Giscard d'Estaing. Both nations had been given eight days to leave the island for good. It was May 1974, and the whole archipelago was on fire with talk of independence.

Fornelli had first appeared a year before, landing on the island with his Tannese wife, and forming an immediate rapport with people from the northern branch of John Frum. He spoke very little Bislama, but was a great actor, able to captivate audiences with liberal use of gesture and symbols borrowed from his military days. In May 1973 between six and eight hundred Tannese gathered to hear him speak. Fornelli told the crowds that progress was unavoidable, and only the big men of kastom could control the island's destiny. He announced the formation of a new party, the UTA, and handed out membership cards. After the meeting he claimed 1300 members for this new movement – a figure tallying mysteriously with the exact number of membership cards he'd had printed.

In March 1974, dressed in white with a natty red paratrooper's beret, Fornelli renamed the UTA Focona (Four Corners) and raised the flag of the Tannese nation. Before an audience of eight hundred, he named leaders to represent the four corners of the movement, north, south, east and west. The eastern leader was a high-up within the Ipeukel-based John Frum. A further meeting was scheduled for 22 June, when Fornelli would be enthroned as chief, and appointed Voice of the Canoe for the new Tannese nation.

Fornelli may have had a large ego, but he was neither a megalomaniac nor a troublemaker. His speeches stressed the friendliness of France, Britain and Australia. As far as he saw it, he was a friend of kastom, trying to organise it on activist lines so that it had a fighting chance, in the oncoming independence process, against the politicised Christians. But the Condominium authorities became seriously afraid that they might lose control over the island. In May 1974 they outlawed the wearing of paramilitary uniforms and the raising of flags. In June the British district agent marched into a Focona stronghold and seized the flag and what was described as weapons but turned out to be a solitary Mauser made in 1916.

Enraged, Fornelli landed on Tanna the next day and sent his declaration of war to Britain and France. In fact, he was making a political bluff – hoping to draw international attention to Tanna's plight. But it was taken seriously in Port Vila – from where the government dispatched forty policemen. They hunted Fornelli and his men in the bush. A peculiar escapade ensued, with gun-toting police pursuing kastom activists armed with bows and arrows. Fortunately, no one was killed. The Tannese leaders, once captured, received jail sentences of a month apiece. Fornelli got eighteen months, and was banned from re-entering the New Hebrides for five years. He flouted this repeatedly, though, returning three times, and referring to himself as King of Tanna right up until his death in 1999.

Meanwhile, as talk of independence gained pace, most New Hebrideans gathered beneath the mast of parties loyal to either the English or the French side of the debate. The archipelago suffered an epidemic of acronyms, mutating by the month, as the NHCA (New Hebrides Cultural Association) became the NHNP (New Hebrides National Party) and finally the VP (Vanuaaku Pati), while the UPNH (Union de la Population des Nouvelles-Hébrides) jostled with the MANH (Mouvement Autonomiste des Nouvelles-Hébrides) and the UCNH (Unions des Communautés des Nouvelles-Hébrides). The political borders followed older routes drawn by religion and language. The group that became the leading VP were largely English-speaking, mission-educated Presbyterians and they followed the British government in seeking a swift independence. They stood in opposition to an assortment of French-speaking, Catholic groups, who wanted a slow handover, or none at all. There were also various kastom-oriented parties, like John Frum on Tanna, who lined up behind the French camp simply because of their dislike of the Presbyterians, and were collectively known as Moderet, or the Moderates.

Once Focona had let them down, the John Frum cultists were ripe to be courted by other parties, in particular the pro-French, anti-independence Moderet block. National elections were held in 1975, 1977 and 1979, with John Frum candidates winning seats each

time as part of Team Moderet. The French republic became benefactors of the messianic movement,
giving them a motorboat and a landcruiser. From the
mid 1970s, the French resident commissioner attended the 15 February ceremony – although in 1978 he
was noticeably miffed to see them raising the Stars and
Stripes, a flag some said had been sent by John Frum,
although it's more likely a passing yachtie donated it.
When he returned in 1980, they had respectfully added
a tricolour to the flags flying at Frum HQ.

The cult leadership had now established the John
Frum Guards, a private police force, which arrested
people for crimes ranging from adultery and sorcery
to pig thieving. The British and French governments
did nothing to stop them. Christian VP supporters and
kastom groups not within the fold viewed the Frum
Guards with dread, seeing them as little more than a
squad of hired goons who went round beating up political opponents.

It became clear that, for all their messianic expec-
tation of a better world to come, the John Frum were
adept at getting a good deal in this one. As the elections approached in 1979, cult leaders shrewdly told
the Moderet representatives they weren't going to vote
at all this time. After all, what was the point, when John
Frum and America were going to look after them?
Alarmed, the French resident commissioner, Inspector General Jean-Jacques Robert, made several trips to

Tanna, handing out cigarettes, rice and tinned food. It worked, but only up to a point. Despite the added weight of the John Frum supporters, it was the VP that gained the majority of votes. Independence was set for 30 July the following year.

In January 1980 some kastom leaders on Tanna declared independence, as part of the new nation of Tafea – another in the rash of acronyms, this time formed by the names of the five participating islands: Tanna, Aneityum, Futuna, Erromango and Aniwa. Rather cheekily, alongside declaring independence, they requested immediate aid from the French government.

But perhaps this wasn't so arrogant, after all. So far as Paris was concerned, a French-funded Tafea would have been much better than an independent, French-hating Vanuatu. A weak state, dependent upon aid, would pose no threat to the nickel-rich lands of nearby New Caledonia, nor raise much objection to that popular Gallic pastime, letting off nuclear bombs in the Pacific. Even so, not much happened, until 26 May, when kastom supporters attacked government offices and kidnapped the newly appointed district commissioner and his deputy. It was rumoured that, shortly before this attack, the head of the French gendarmerie had departed the island and left his keys and a full tank of petrol in the vehicle the kidnappers used to spirit their captives away. The next day the Condominium's Joint

Mobile Force flew to Tanna and engaged the rebels. Tafea supporters tried to dynamite the invaders but were routed with teargas. The two captured officials escaped. Thirty men were arrested and jailed. Relative calm returned to the island.

So were the French secretly backing Tafea? Someone certainly was – and the main culprit began to emerge from the shadows as more uprisings rocked the larger, central island of Santo. Since the sixties there'd been a thriving kastom community up there, organised by a charismatic, half-Scottish Santoese named Jimmy Stephens. They called themselves Nagriamel, they wanted the Europeans off their lands, and they had even visited the UN, in New York, to petition for independence.

On the same day as the Tanna revolt began, Jimmy Stephens's Nagriamel supporters attacked the offices of the VP in town. Like Tafea, Nagriamel had declared independence – again – in January of that year, now calling itself the nation of Vemerana.

The two revolts had obviously been co-ordinated, and the finger pointed in a strange direction. Back in 1968 Michael Oliver, a Lithuanian escapee from the concentration camps, had published a book entitled *A New Constitution for A New Country*. Heavily influenced by far-right politics, this Nevada businessman started buying up land in the Pacific. On one trip, in 1971, Oliver had met Jimmy Stephens, and subsequently became his adviser. In June 1975, along with various American businessmen who felt their country was heading towards destruction, Oliver formed the Phoenix Foundation. Their aim was to create a libertarian utopia free from government interference. In 1972 and 1975 they made abortive attempts to establish their stateless state in Tonga and the Bahamas.

They then switched their sights to Santo – funding Jimmy Stephens on his UN visit in 1976. Nagriamel declared self-sovereignty several times that year, with Oliver acting as adviser behind the scenes. It was also rumoured the Phoenix Foundation was providing weapons, ammunition and equipment for a pirate radio station. In May of the following year the Phoenix rose again, offering plots of Santoese land for sale on two-hundred-year leases. A constitution was created, one suitably amenable to gun-runners, paedophiles, crackpots and drugs barons, and Oliver funded the production of gold and silver coins, with Jimmy Stephens's head on them. Pamphlets were published, introducing the 'Nagriamel Federation' as a country without taxes, and a government that left you alone. And similar pamphlets were circulating on Tanna.

The Vemerana revolt on Santo proved quite successful – with its supporters kidnapping the government's representative and occupying the main town. VP members fled, along with British and Australians, whose governments had urged them to get out. Vemerana held the town for two months, until the British and French finally managed to agree to the extent of sending troops. Meanwhile the islands of Malekula, Aoba and Ambrym all declared independence too.

Meanwhile, on Tanna, the turmoil continued, as Tafea supporters marched on the police headquarters to demand the release of their comrades. Government militia and VP vigilantes faced a mob of various Moderet groups – who were, just to make things crystal clear, opposed to independence, but wanted independence in order to be dependent on France. Shots were fired, the prisoners broke free, and in the confusion a prominent leader from the John Frum camp, Alexis Iolu, was killed.

An official enquiry never uncovered who fired the fatal shot. Meanwhile the government acted swiftly to punish those who'd been involved in the rebellion. An Irish priest who objected to the rebels' treatment was expelled from Tanna. A French admiral who'd been overseeing secret channels of support to Tafea was stripped of his position. (With a stroke of bureaucratic irony, he was made naval attaché to the land-locked central African nation of Chad.)

Oliver's libertarianism and John Frum's ideology were made for one another. For Phoenix, Tanna offered the territory for a utopian state. For the Tafea–John Frum leaders, Phoenix offered money and logistical support. But there was also a mystical angle, because this aid came from America, home of their god, John Frum. There was a fatal attraction between the mindsets of these two very different groups. The hero of libertarianism is the rugged individual, who through his own qualities of canniness and hard graft, is able to stand out from the crowd. Ditto the 'Big Man' on Tanna, and throughout Melanesia. Encounters with Big Men, with their enthusiasm for amassing pigs, their eloquence in debate, their ceaseless pursuit of personal progress, had so entranced American anthropologist Marshall Sahlins in 1963 that he described them as 'thoroughly bourgeois, so reminiscent of the free-wheeling rugged individual of our own heritage'.

The Frum–Phoenix love affair, of course, also slotted into far older and deep-rooted Tannese ideas about reuniting the island with some distant land mass. But amid the frantic canvassing and alliance switching of the pre-independence years, this symbolic road building turned into a tangible political process, as well as remaining a spiritual one. When the Norwegian anthropologist Øystein Vigestad was on the island in the late seventies, he described the men of the Yaohnanen area watching their neighbours askance. They saw them belly-diving into dangerous alliances with French diplomats, Corsican rebels and shadowy conglomerates of American-based businessmen, and either thriving or losing out in an unpredictable fashion. At the same time, as everyone else lined up behind one flag or figurehead to march into the battle, they must have been wondering: who was theirs?

Just as I was about to leave the airport building and walk out onto the sunlit tarmac, I felt a tap on my shoulder, and turned round to see Nako. Having grabbed my attention, he looked sheepishly down to the rubber tips of his newly acquired deck shoes, an awkward air about him that urged me, suddenly and forcefully, to forgive everything.

He'd done a lot for me, after all, this short, battered little man, and I was wrong to leave him without thanks. What, in the end, had he really done wrong? Tell the odd fib. Try to big himself up, get back in his dad's good books. Had it prevented me from learning what I'd come here to learn?

'Thank you for everything, Nako.'

He looked up. 'Your watch,' he said, fixing me with a bloodshot eye. 'You said I could have your watch.'

Numbly, I started to take it off. 'Also that aftershave potion,' he added.

Later, as if he'd now retreated to a specimen under a magnifying glass, I watched him through the tiny window of the aeroplane. His father's final words had been an attack on greed. Nako's finals words to me had been, just like all his others, concerned, primarily, with Nako. And in their separate ways, the two crystallised what it meant to be Man Tanna. To deplore greed, and at the same time fight a lifelong fight for the honours due a Big Man. To seek harmony and balance, and still ensure it's your village which gets the road, the truck, the water tap and the tourists. Perhaps we were just as contradictory. In the name of fairness and tolerance, we poured scorn on Philip – not seeming to see that we weren't fair to him, or to the Tannese.

Chief Jack Naiva died in 2010, but the movement continues, now headed by his grandson, Siko Nathuan. It seems to have drifted, or perhaps been concertedly driven, away from Naiva's stripped-back, private pietism, towards a more extrovert kind of religious expression. There are now shrines in the village, a Union Jack flies, and the villagers dance on the Duke of Edinburgh's birthday. They may be doing this to compete with the symbols and ceremonies of their neighbours. They may also have realised that if film-makers and journalists are going to keep coming, then they need something concrete to film and photograph. And it works. The newsmen still come, and over time the coverage has become gentler, although that has more to do with etiquette than understanding. There's a po-faced earnestness about anyone we perceive to live in a 'tribe' nowadays, but that doesn't stop us talking utter hogwash about them. The *Vancouver Courier*, for example, has the people of Yaohnanen longing for bottles of Coke. The *Christian Science Monitor* dates the movement to a visit made by the Queen and Prince Philip in 1971, which never happened. Britain's *Daily Mail* says

Chief Jack's 'tribe' expects cargo to fall from the sky. Philippism may sound like nonsense, but a lot of the material written about it is more so.

All newspaper descriptions of Chief Jack Naiva accentuated his age, or the fact that he was never entirely sure about it, or the isolation of his settlement. They seemed blind to his interest in world affairs, or his chiefly bearing or the love his village bore for him. After his death we have continued to see the people of his village – usually described erroneously as 'the Yaohnanen', or 'the Yaohnanen tribe' – like forlorn commuters, stranded for ever at some windy bus stop, craning their necks for a sign of the redemption that never comes. No article mentions how full and rich and free their lives are, how much spare time they have for simple pleasures. That waiting for Prince Philip is not the irksome, painful process of longing we would make it, but something they simply slot into their daily experience.

A few lines in one newspaper unwittingly sum it all up:

'"You must tell King Philip that I'm getting old and I want him to come and visit me before I die," said the white-haired chief, who thinks he is about 80. "If he can't come perhaps he could send us something: a Land Rover, bags of rice or a little money."'

A thorough piece, but its writer failed to notice, even in the midst of an article linking the Prince Philip movement to cargo cults, how unconcerned about cargo Chief Jack was. 'If he can't come perhaps he could send us something.' Hardly the mud-encrusted savage, praying for some divine tornado of Coke bottles and toasters. The Chief's words echoed what he'd said when I asked him about cargo – that, of course, Prince Philip would bring gifts, because he was a rich man. But that wasn't the point. Just as I fear I did, with my blundering around after shrines and snooping on imaginary myth stealers, everyone who has visited the Philippists has somehow missed the point. And probably because the Philippists wanted them to.

And what was the point? Perhaps it's this: that after two hundred years of bewildering contact with whites, and amid the melee of pre-independence politics, the people of Yaohnanen needed some road, symbolic and real, towards an outside power. Since the end of Wolwatu it had seemed like some new type of white man was coming to Tanna. Men like rough and ready photographer Karl Müller, friendly, plain-speaking trader Bob Paul, anthropologists Kirk Huffman and Jean Guiart, attentive and respectful of kastom. But after 1966 this trend appeared to be coming to an end. Unwittingly, government representative Alexander Wilkie created a spiritual crisis by not returning the pig.

Divining, as they so often did, historical phases through symbol, metaphor and wordplay, the people of Yaohnanen saw the small breach of pig-swapping protocol as an augur. A man called Mr Wilkes had come before, and then given way to the unpopular Mr Nichol, who'd imprisoned those who rose to John Frum's flag. Decades on, Mr Wilkie's tiny blunder, forgetting to reciprocate a gift, threatened to usher in a new age in which kastom was blocked. Anxieties intensified as, all around them, fellow Tannese forged meaningful roads with helpful foreign powers.

When the Norwegian anthropologist Øystein Vigestad spent time with the Philippists at the close of the seventies, he described a place at once bucolic and anxious. Up on the mountain tops of Yaohnanen, isolated by geography, and therefore off the itinerary of most political types, kastom life continued in rhythms millennia old. At the same time, from this vantage point, men like Chief Naiva and Tuk Noao could gaze down to the fray below and see two things happening. Their John Frum and Christian neighbours, in more accessible areas, were gaining obvious advantages as the lines were drawn for the newly independent state. At the same time, the more their fellow Tannese flirted with France and America and Britain, the more of their kastom they lost.

Prince Philip was their perfect solution: battle-standard, source of income, symbol and personal friend. It was obvious these alliances with whites were risky. Phoenix and Fornelli had let Man Tanna down. Amer-

ica and Jesus Christ had failed to deliver on the promises made by John Frum prophets and the missionaries. Friendly whites had come before – there'd been Golovnin, the sympathetic traders Humes and Truss, who'd stood with Man Tanna against the missionaries – but in each case they'd been replaced by their opposites.

Prince Philip could never let them down, nor turn into a hostile type of white, because he didn't belong to France, or England, or America or any of the other nations the Tannese knew. Their conversations with Jean Guiart had confirmed for them what they wanted to hear, that he was from Tanna, some avatar of the light-skinned god, probably the imported Polynesian garden spirit Mwatiktik, whom they'd known for centuries.

Their belief – or their strategy – was shored up by Philip's own conduct. In 1971 the Duke came to the northern part of the archipelago, intending to fly a plane from his ship to the village of Lakatoro on Malekula. A hurricane prevented this, but what Philip lost in adventure, he gained in publicity, as the regional press picked up on the story of the dashing princely pilot. News of this trickled down to Tanna, where some people already believed John Frum would be returning one day, from America, by aeroplane. It was now mooted that Philip might be piloting it. Pictures of his eventual walkabout on Lakatoro show him in naval whites, with brass buttons – eerily like the early descriptions of John Frum.

But of more importance than the mythological angle was Philip's own attitude. He has, in recent years, appeared like a bored teenager on foreign junkets: yawning at the tribal dancing, trying to liven things up with the odd howler. But this Pacific circuit showed a very different Prince. Unencumbered by his wife, Mrs Queen, and accompanied by his favourite maternal uncle, Louis Mountbatten, for Philip this was Lads On Tour, with gold knobs on. Sometimes he wore a Hawaiian shirt – just like the bush boys do when they're living the high life in Port Vila. He swam in lagoons, rubbed noses with Tahitian lovelies, sat grinning on a plastic chair chalked with the word 'throne'.

Pictures of that time show a relaxed, happy man, someone deeply into the stuff he's seeing. The Pacific spoke to something within Philip – its respect for the sea, its manly values, its gruff, hearty, unpretentious ways. Perhaps it also reminded him of the first place he'd felt at home. After years of semi-orphan status in the chilly castles of Europe, he found a proper family in the bowels of a battle cruiser. He stoked the furnaces when the Chinese crew jumped ship. He paid a little girl in chocolate bars to scrub the barnacles off the rails, and decades later, on an official visit to Hong Kong, went and looked her up. The warm side of Philip came out at sea, and never more so than among the islands of the South Pacific. That's why, just three years after this first visit, he dragged the whole royal circus back, this time with wife and daughter in tow.

It's also significant that on Malekula the Duke ceremonially, symbolically killed a pig, thereby being made 'Lokorimal Bwatenvenu', Chief of All the Islands, a top-ranking rung on the nimangki Big Man ladder. There was no such title on Tanna, but the Duke's attitude, summed up in his willingness to get the royal hands dirty in a ritual, was known, and appreciated. Here was no awkward official, the likes of whom they'd seen so many over the years. When men like Chief Jack Naiva sailed out to greet Philip on his second trip, they saw an imposing figure of white and bronze and silver, who'd already proven his friendliness to kastom.

A whole cosmology flowed into and out of this perceived friendship: the older idea of black and white men as separated brothers, the mystical concept of a shattered cosmos, with people and continents split apart from their other halves. So Philip, Duke of Edinburgh, and hence the overlord of Hebrides Old and New, served a purpose both spiritual and political. As a man combining bronze and silver, Tanna and England, black and white, he embodied the process they longed for. By seeking a road with him, they attracted further friendly white visitors: journalists, camera crews, tourists, government men, confirming the idea that Philip could unite people of different skins, maybe unite everything exiled from itself. Vigestad's account of his time on Tanna had villagers enthusing about the changing landscape as much as worrying about it: people saw signs of increasing closeness everywhere – marriages of black and white, mixed race children, Melanesians employing white men, and they readily attributed it to their magical doings of their own, black-and-white mountain god, Philip.

Philippism was Yaohnanen's way of defining and keeping a political identity in uncertain times. It had something none of their neighbours' schemes had: a backer both foreign and home-grown at the same time. It also had authenticity: Philip wasn't just alive and walking around in a way that Jesus and John Frum weren't: he sent letters and photographs to prove his mutual interest in the road.

His cult also basked in the distinction of being utterly unlike Christianity, or John Frum, or any other movement that seemed to have failed. Without prayers or hymns or paraphernalia, it could be practised secretly and constantly – in and through the daily business of living the traditional lifestyle. It had no symbols to attack, or burn down or ban. Strangers and snoopers need not even know that Philippism was being practised under their noses. By simply staying true to kastom, you worshipped your god.

The cult is so impeccably Tannese, so shot through with their turbulent history and their harmonious worldview, that it's easy to lose sight of its very European figurehead. But the people of Yaohnanen never do. Letters continue to pass back and forth between Buckingham Palace and the Pacific. In 1980, as the newly founded government of Vanuatu tried to impose a head tax throughout the archipelago, the Philippists asked their Patron Prince to intercede. Philip wrote back, telling them to pay up – but for years afterwards, unable to read, Chief Jack waved the letter in the face of government men, convinced he had Buckingham Palace backing. Ever since then, newspaper articles have been collected, pored over and preserved. Philip-related trivia – his date of birth, the names of his grandchildren – are treasured and swapped in those nakamals where his name is sacred. He was adopted for political reasons, perhaps, but his Tannese parents are no less interested in the real man.

So what does Philip make of it? Contrary to what our own myths tell us, Philip has always been an innovator within the Royal Family. He cut costs throughout the various households. He replaced logistically tricky plane flights with cheaper, more convenient helicopters. In a milieu where some traditions date back to William the Conqueror, he has been seen as a radical. Most radically, and ironically, of all, it was Philip who sought to harness the power of the media. He was the first royal to be interviewed on television. Eight years afterwards, in 1969, twenty-three million viewers tuned in to watch an intimate portrait of Royal Family life, an idea conceived and campaigned for by Philip. But even if he approves of openness, he has stayed quiet about the cult. When I approached the Palace with my own questions, I was answered, but any probings as to the Prince's personal feelings drew a witheringly regal silence.

He has, at last, met men from Tanna. Just as Chief Jack predicted, after my return to England I was a 'gate' for a brief, partially televised union of worshippers and worshipped. I'd acted as adviser to a TV crew, bringing a group of kastom people over to experience the British way of life, and as an extra treat, a meeting at Windsor had gone onto the itinerary. 'How are your gardens?' was the black-and white god's opening gambit to the Tannese delegation. Nobody fainted, and since the footage has been shown on Tanna, nobody has slaughtered all their pigs or thrown their money into the volcano. Prince Philip played the perfect royal host: friendly, manly, slightly distant. He didn't give much away. Nor did he make any of his famous faux pas about pot bellies or cannibals.

But Prince Philip only lets these little shockers loose when he is bored. 'Where is the machine that shrinks things?' he once said while being shown around a laundry. And any man who can come up with a witticism when he's being shown around a laundry is a figure to admire. The same is true for most, but not all of his jokes. 'No wonder you're deaf if you stand next to that,' he said, listening to a steel band performance at a school for the hard of hearing. Outrage greeted that comment, and yet, at exactly the same time, sitcoms on our worthiest TV channels probed subjects such as disability and sexuality for a bit of a giggle.

The world doesn't need to feel sorry for Philip, but it ought to recognise that he, and we, play our parts on a wider field. Just like the Tannese in the pre-independence years, we live in an age of quicksand values. A word or a joke permissible last decade renders its user a pariah now. So a personality like Philip acts as a pressure valve. With his murky origins and his dubious status, he is not just tabu, not just a figure of loathing, but also one of licence. Like the Jester, the only personage permitted in medieval times to fart at the nobles and tweak their noses, Philip has the freedom to make the comments we no longer dare to. He is the perfect post-war Mr Punch: we can experience the illicit thrill of enjoying his comments at the same time as condemning them. Just as the Tannese did, with their symbol of a mixed-race kastom prince, we can have our cake and eat it. Philip is as useful to us as he is to them.

It's odd, though, that this modern, post-colonial monarch, equipped with a Press Secretary, keenly aware of his bilious relations with the media, would have encouraged a group of impoverished, black-skinned former subjects to believe something that wasn't true. Yes, they probably would have carried on believing it anyway, but the Palace didn't have to send photographs and letters to encourage them. It could so easily have turned into a PR disaster for the Prince – been seen at best as a gesture with ill-conceived consequences, at worst as a faintly racist trick.

He went along with it because kastom and Philip were as suited as John Frum and Phoenix. He admired the Melanesian Big Man-type, with his self-reliance and his forthright manners, because that's the type of man he was. He went along with it because, bearing in mind the mess being left behind by the hastily imploding Empire, his diplomatic advisers in London and Port Vila argued that a friendly gesture was preferable to no gesture at all. And lastly, Prince Philip went along with it, probably, because he found it as amusing as we do.

It's more than that, of course – and, to the Tannese, something entirely different. We should recognise that, but it doesn't cancel out our own right, for our own reasons, to appreciate its ironies. A Prince, seen by us as a bigot, adopted by black people as a symbol of enduring racial harmony. A figure surrounded by wealth, obscured by ceremony, yet somehow revered in a place which embraced simplicity. A man excluded from politics, made a masthead for a people who did nothing but politics all day. A joke to one group, a powerful faith for another.

My last glimpse of Nako was of him, pressed like a little boy against the wire fence as the plane rose into the sky. It was an emblem for his life, I thought, hanging on, waiting for some personal take-off, at the edge of the runway, but never quite there. We levelled out over a sea the colour of paintings, and I wiped the dusty smudge where my watch used to be. Presently a stewardess handed out tiny glasses of orange squash, and I seized mine with the greed of the newly freed, tipping its luxuriously European contents straight into my mouth. My neighbour proffered a bag of crisps and I happily shoved a handful of them in, as well. They remained, frozen in a liminal phase, as my tastebuds detected a sooty, cardboardy tang.

'Made of yams,' my neighbour said proudly. 'Do you like them?'

'Erghmgh.'

'They have many kinds of yams on Tanna, you know. But not as many as my island. On my island, we have a black yam and a stone yam and a snake yam and a yam that's big as a house...'

Glossary

Ambrym: island in the northern Vanuatu archipelago; the site during World War Two of cultic activity, allegedly spread by John Frum supporters from Tanna.

Aneityum/Anatom: island south of Tanna, visited by Prince Philip on his second tour of the region in 1974.

Aore and Aoba: islands in the northern Vanuatu archipelago.

bêche-de-mer: French name for the sea-slug or abalone, high demand for which in China drew the first white traders to the New Hebrides area.

Big Man: the archetypal Melanesian leader, dependent for his prestige on pigs, visions, magical abilities, charisma, political clout, speech-making.

Bislama   (pronounced   *BISH-la-ma*):   English-based

pidgin, originally developed by sea-slug traders and now the official language of Vanuatu.

blackbirding: the 'recruiting', sometimes by force or deception, of Melanesian labour for European-owned mines and plantations across the Pacific region.

cargo cult: movement found in a number of Pacific settings from the 1880s to the present day, with characteristics including but not limited to: millenarian expectations, anti-colonial feeling, rejection of Western forms of Christianity, revival of old traditions, copying of Western customs, desire for, and making preparations to receive, imported, factory-made Western goods.

Condominium: joint government of the New Hebrides by Britain and France, 1906–80. Sometimes called the Pandemonium.

Cook, Captain James: famous British explorer and the first European to arrive on Tanna, on 30 July 1774.

De Quirós, Pedro Fernández: Portuguese explorer, who crossed the South Pacific in 1605–6 in search of Australia and was the first European to arrive in the New Hebrides.

Efate: large island, the most populous in the Vanuatu

archipelago and containing the capital, Port Vila; home to a major US military base during World War Two.

Erromango: island immediately north of Tanna; its population was drastically reduced by contact with Westerners.

Futuna: small Polynesian island at the southern tip of the Vanuatu archipelago; possibly the place of origin of Tanna's garden god Mwatiktik.

Focona: pro-kastom movement founded on Tanna in the 1970s by Antoine Fornelli (see 'kastom' and 'Fornelli, Antoine').

Fornelli, Antoine: Corsican-born former Foreign Legionnaire and plantation owner who encouraged kastom-led revolts in the years leading up to the New Hebrides' gaining of independence as Vanuatu in 1980.

Fred, aka Fred Nase, aka Prophet Fred: Tannese spiritual leader, whose Unity movement encourages a kastom-ised Christianity.

Frum, John (sometimes also Jon Brum or Broom): prophetic figure emerging as a revolt against mission Christianity in 1940s Tanna; sometimes said to be a US airman, and now the Messiah figure in a seventy-year-old cult on the island.

German Wislun: anti-British cult which emerged in Papua New Guinea at the start of World War One.

Golovnin, Vasili Mikhailovich (1776–1831): Russian navigator, who spent time on Tanna in July 1809.

Guiart, Jean: French anthropologist and campaigner for exiled John Frum activists.

Huffman, Kirk: anthropologist, honorary curator of the Vanuatu Kaljoral Senta in Port Vila, and now based in Sydney.

Ielgis Iakukkak Iapnamal, Iatanas, Ioknaauka: kastom villages in south-west Tanna, near to Yaohnanen.

Kal: one of Chief Jack Naiva's sons, named after the photographer Karl Müller, who worked on Tanna in the 1970s.

Kalbaben (also Karaperamun or Karapenmun): god of Mount Tukosmwera on Tanna, and said to be Prince Philip's father.

kastom: from the Bislama word for 'custom'; traditional

Melanesian beliefs, ways of life, ceremonies, dress, food and artefacts; many kastom people strongly oppose schooling, Christianity, politics, the monetary economy and urban living.

kava: *Piper methysticum,* narcotic root related to the pepper plant, drunk for ritual and ceremonial purposes throughout the Pacific. And for getting smashed.

kleva: a traditional magician, seer, prophet or sorcerer.

Lomakom: Christian-educated former teacher resident on Tanna; kastom sceptic and general thorn in the side.

Malekula: island in the northern Vanuatu archipelago; visited by Prince Philip on his 1971 tour.

Mwatiktik: Tannese food god – possibly derived from the Polynesian Maui-tiki-tiki-tao-a-taranga – described as pale-skinned and a relative of Kalbaben, god of the local mountain, Tukosmwera. He could be part of the mythological basis for Philip worship.

Nagriamel: independence-seeking kastom movement on the northern Vanuatu island of Santo, led by Jimmy Stephens and funded by Phoenix (see 'Oliver, Michael').

Naiva, Chief Jack: chief of Yaohnanen village in south-west Tanna and, at the time of the author's visit, the last surviving founder member of the Philip cult. Died in 2009.

nakamal: meeting/dancing/ritual space outside Tannese villages.

Nako: Chief Jack Naiva's son, and the author's guide on Tanna.

Nakwa: a serpent god, often identified with Satan, or a Frenchman, and considered to be responsible for money, politics and wet dreams.

nalnal: a carved club used for killing pigs and for ceremonial purposes.

nambas: penis cover made of a dried pandanus leaf.

Nasabl: a son of the god Kalbaben; in myths he protects Tanna from the flood.

Nauvhal (also known in south-west Tanna as Nifaa): language spoken in the Yaohnanen area.

Nimangki: grade-taking ceremonies on Malekula island, participated in by Prince Philip, in which would-be Big

Men ascend the rungs of kastom society by obtaining and donating pigs to those above them.

Oliver, Michael: concentration-camp survivor and later Nevada businessman behind the Phoenix Foundation, funding independence movements on Tanna and Santo in the hope of creating a libertarian utopia.

Tafea: acronym formed from the names of five neighbouring islands in southern Vanuatu – Tanna, Aneityum, Futuna, Erromango and Aniwa – and adopted by the short-lived Tafea Republic in 1980.

Tuk Noao: seer and spokesman for the Prince Philip cult at the time of its birth in the 1940s, contemporary of Chief Jack Naiva, and carver of the famous nalnal sent to Prince Philip.

Yakel: thriving kastom village and tourist destination, led, at the time of the author's visit, by Chief Johnson Kowiya.

Yaohnanen: HQ of the Prince Philip cult, and one of the twelve great villages of Tanna said to have been ordained by the gods.

Wunghen: Tannese creator god.

Acknowledgements and Apologies

THIS book owes thanks to many people, all over the world – especially those on Tanna, and in particular the inhabitants of Yaohnanen and surrounding villages. (I should add that I've changed the names and physical appearance of some of the people I met on my visit to the island.) In Port Vila, everyone at the Vanuatu Kaljoral Senta was enormously helpful, and without the assistance of Jakob Kaprere, Ann Naupa and Ralph Regenvanu, I would never have made my trip. Kirk Huffman and his wife Yvonne Carillo-Huffman provided, and continue to provide, years of advice, support and friendship. I am also indebted to the personal communications of a number of Tanna experts, especially Lamont Lindstrom and Øystein Vigestad, and to the ideas and information contained in the following, far better-researched books and articles:

The Blackbirders: A Brutal Story of the Kanaka Slave

Trade, Edward Wybergh Docker, Angus & Robertson, 1981.

Cargo Cult: Strange Stories of Desire From Melanesia and Beyond, Lamont Lindstrom, South Sea Books, University of Hawa'i Press, Honolulu, 1993.

'Cult and Culture: American Dreams in Vanuatu', Lamont Lindstrom, *Pacific Studies*, IV:2 (Spring 1981), p104.

Duke of Hazard: The Wit and Wisdom of Prince Philip, Phil Dampier and Ashley Walton, Book Guild Ltd, 2006.

Island Encounters: Black and White Memories of the Pacific War, Lamont Lindstrom (with G.M. White), Smithsonian Institution Press, 1990.

John Frum, He Come, Edward Rice, Doubleday, 1974.

Lengten etter Paradiset: om 'kastom' rørsla: ei nativistisk, politisk-religiøs rørsle på Tanna, Vanuatu, Øystein Vigestad, University of Oslo, 1984.

Philip and Elizabeth: Portrait of a Royal Marriage, Gyles Brandreth, Arrow, 2005.

Prince Philip: A Biography, Denis Judd, Time Warner Paperbacks, 1991.

Prince Philip: A Family Portrait, Alexandra, Queen of Yugoslavia, Hodder & Stoughton, 1959.

Savage Civilisation, Tom Harrison, Left Book Club/Gollancz, 1937.

'Spitting on Tanna', Monty Lindstrom, *Oceania*, vol. 50, no. 3 (March 1980), pp228–34.

To Kill A Bird With Two Stones, Jeremy McClancy, Vanuatu Cultural Centre, 2002.

The Tree and the Canoe: History and Ethnogeography of Tanna, Joel Bonnemaison, University of Hawai'i Press, 1994.

The Trumpet Shall Sound, Peter Worsley, McGibbon & Kee, 1957.

Un Siècle et Demi de Contacts Culturels à Tanna, Nouvelles-Hébrides, Jean Guiart, Office de la Recherche Scientifique et Technique d'Outre-Mer, 1956.

The Duke: Portrait of Prince Philip, Tim Heald, Hodder & Stoughton, 1991.

Tufala Gavman: Reminiscences from the Anglo-French Condominium of the New Hebrides, Brian J. Bresnihan and Keith Woodward (eds.), Institute of Pacific Studies, 2002.

I apologise for any sources I may have omitted from the list above; to anyone I may have forgotten to thank; for any errors I've made; and, most of all, for any offence I may have accidentally caused while on Tanna or in describing it here. This includes flouting the rules of Bislama spelling in the book's title, which should properly be *Man Blong Missis Kwin*, and in numerous instances throughout the book, in the interests of aiding readers' comprehension of a tongue that sounds very like English but is often spelt very differently.

More generally, I do not claim to have 'tracked

down' anything in a place where ideas and interpretations flow as freely as the kava. At least one, very knowledgeable source told me it was a New Zealand teacher who showed the islanders pictures of Prince Philip in a book, and not the anthropologist Jean Guiart. Others, on and off the island, doubt whether any pale-faced Polynesian yam gods had any part in the story. As Chief Jack said at the end of my stay, 'Our thing isn't like that, it's alive and it is moving.' And if that's right, I merely took a snapshot of Philippism at one point in its journey.